SECOND CENTURY MODERNISM

John Jennifer Marx

ORO EDITIONS

TABLE OF CONTENTS

TABLE OF CONTENTS

POEM 1
The universe is expanding.

Balance
is one of the most fundamental
and least understood aspects
of the inner
and outer world we live in.
We are in a constant state
of readjustment.
toward technology
toward aging
toward finding contentment

Imagine,
trying to make progress,
high on a tightrope,
blindfolded,
navigating by a sense of smell,
without being able to assume which direction is forward

all while
there are winds coming from multiple directions,
trying to blow you off
that precarious wire.
differing concerns,
desires,
responsibilities

This can describe the life condition of any of us.

REBALANCING
MODERNISM

It could be said that Walter Gropius laid the cornerstone of modern architecture in 1919 by founding the Bauhaus. As a result, modern architecture is now over 100 years old. This first century of modernism has come to a close with a mixed review. Enthusiasm for its achievements goes hand in hand with a discontent about a sizable portion of its outcome, as well as its effect on the natural and built environments. The most vocal supporters of these modernist ideals crafted epic claims that modernism was bound to deliver progressive and humane environments. Alas, the follow-through of those promises was uneven at best.

Bauhaus Dessau, 1925–1926, Walter Gropius, photograph by Lucia Moholy

Can we update this ideological framework, establishing a new outlook that is both open-ended and operational? If the first century of modernism can be considered an architecture of abstraction and ideas, then what might we design if we turn our attention, in this second century of modernism, to an architecture of emotional abundance? Second Century Modernism creates an architecture of richness and community by placing a higher priority on emotional meaning, through a shift in the design process that balances the rational with the intuitive, and a "Less + More" approach to expanding the range of cultural values we can inclusively balance in our environments. It welcomes you to embrace the paradoxical qualities of human existence.

First Century Modernism
The promises made by "First Century Modernism" are still worthy of being fulfilled, but a fundamental aspect has eroded in the past 60 years. Indeed, a cornerstone of purpose in architecture is the capacity to affect human emotions, to lift the human spirit. This is what creates the bonds that make societies strong. Modern architecture, in countless manifestos written during the avant-garde period, did help give a programmatic direction to architectural action in the 20th century. Alas, in the myriad of design languages that were produced in that short time frame, modern architecture shines in far too few occasions, especially when compared to the global production of banal and mundane buildings.

What followed was postmodernism, a mannerist period made palatable with irony. It offered a retreat from the collective alarm toward a raging modernity in the built environment, but resulted in a questionable architectural outcome that was short-lived when compared

Piazza del Campo, Siena, Italy

Seoul, South Korea

to the models it was referencing. While great progress was made in raising the consciousness about the link between architecture and the emotional reaction of the general public, it fell short in providing the rich environments that create community. In many ways, the theories behind postmodernism created a compelling goal, but did not go deep enough in terms of understanding how form affects culture and how the foundational processes by which we think about design—and how we actually design—had become out of balance with the goal of creating humane environments.

Second Century Modernism is an alternative to both First Century Modernism and postmodernism. It emanates from those original promises, but does so with a particular strategy: it creates an architecture of abundance and embraces paradox.

An Architecture of Abundance
Three dramatic shifts are required for Second Century Modernism to become a tangible architectural reality:

1. Emotional Meaning and Cultural Vibrancy need to be primary determinants of design, in concert with the current hegemony of concept and function. Emotional Meaning in architecture occurs when the elements or the character of a space arouse an emotional response in the user that is meaningful, significant, and enduring. This can span a wide range of emotions: "does an environment feel safe, welcoming, hopeful, or beautiful" or is it "oppressive, heavy, alienating, or empty"?

Cultural Vibrancy is the sum of individual contributions pertaining to the enrichment of human experience beyond attending to basic needs and given in urban settlements and rural settings where a sense of the collective is perceived. It is the sense of joy that makes life worth living with others that comes from the arts and social rituals that make up that culture.

2. The Design Process and the Priorities embedded within it need to change. For most of First Century Modernism, we emphasized the verbal over the visual, the mind over the heart. The intuitive was branded as arbitrary and superficial. There are severe limitations that occur when we work with an exclusively linear, rational, and verbal thought process. Second Century Modernism balances that with a three-dimensional, intuitive, and visual creative process.

3. Expanding the Range of Cultural Values inclusively balances our environments through a *Less + More* approach, which reconciles and harmonizes seemingly paradoxical conflicts between conceptual issues, such as:

Thought Process + Creative Process
Concept + Emotional Meaning
Pragmatic + Lyrical
Local + Global
Refinement + Innovation
Arbitrary + Rational
Individual + Community
Restraint + Richness
History + Zeitgeist

Second Century Modernism, therefore, stands for the expansion of the architectural vocabulary to elicit a range of emotionally meaningful responses to the act of building and experiencing architecture. Second Century Modernism represents a new era in architectural action, where design is technologically advanced, aware of its lasting impact on the quality of people's lives, and emotionally meaningful to its users. Second Century Modern architecture conveys a sense of geographical and cultural identity and exhibits poetic ambition.

Less + More
Steeped in digital technology, connectivity, and communication, the architecture of this new century is committed to providing tailored responses to the enormous sociocultural texture of our world today; it embraces the wider spectrum of the human ecosystem. Rather than considering an either/or condition, it moves forward toward a both/and condition. It brings poetry back into design.

Following First Century Modernism, it has become clear that the world that architects design for is multidimensional, complex, layered, and inherently hybrid. Coming from a century of conceptual absolutes and irreconcilable polarities, Second Century Modernism promotes designing in a paradox of perceived opposites. This mode builds on the legacy of Mies van der Rohe's famed principle of

Luminous Moon Gate, Form4 Architecture

"Less + More equates to a design proposition thriving on the diversity of needs, desires, and ambition"

"Less is More," and particularly on the momentum of Dieter Rams's "Less and More" design philosophy, a progressive step toward this fertile openness.[1] *Less and More* remained, nonetheless, a clever version of the Modernist minimalism that brought about mixed results.

Second Century Modernism espouses the notion of "Less + More," where the concept of abundance—which should be differentiated from historicist opulence—is evocative of positive associations in design. This dictate makes of that paradox the entry point into a world that, through a First Century Modernist lens, may appear fractured, illogical, and irreconcilable. Hence the paradox. What is the driver of any design in the presence of such apparent contradiction? *Less + More* equates to a design proposition thriving on the diversity of needs, desires, and ambition. And, in turn, it promotes a creative response to the enormous spectrum of human possibilities.

The pioneers of First Century Modernism invoked purposeful detachment from the reliance on bygone models of canonized classical beauty. Historicism had engulfed architecture with a plethora of references that had imploded by the mid-nineteenth century. Something had to be done. Editing—the shedding of historicism from the art of building—became the most trusted tool for the growing number of hardliners. Through editing, a vast array of elemental compositions could be made expressive in their stylistic nakedness. It worked, for a while. That abstraction, elegant and informed at the onset, later got transformed into a form of unfortunate nonpoetic emptiness. Restraint gave way to poverty of ideas, and modernism reached a tipping point when it became the rule for new construction.

The revolt against the impoverishment of the character of current cities is even more remarkable considering that red light to

[1] https://us.gestalten.com/products/less-and-more-dieter-rams

Eugène Viollet-le-Duc, Paris Opera House, 1861

modernism came straight from the masses it was supposed to serve. Urban blight was the recurring outcome of designing within the strict modernist formula. Loss of character, loss of a sense of place, loss of regional identity, and so forth, are the indirect casualties of a modernist architecture accepted without questioning.

There are marked differences between postmodernism and Second Century Modernism. The former was reactive to a perceived decline of the built environment based on strict urban planning principles rooted in the heroic avant-garde of First Century Modernism. The latter is a synthesis of the sustainable universals that First Century Modernism uncovered in its subversive stance against the classical past, with the earnest assessment of what type of spatial conditions this subversive ethos generated when it shunned foundational critical lessons from the preindustrial past. Postmodernism made of history a stylistic all-you-can-eat buffet purporting a panache it never delivered in built form. Second Century Modernism, by contrast, capitalizes on the realizations of the pioneers of the modern movement that architecture, technology, and space are deeply interconnected in addressing conditions of our time. This new movement builds on the precious reflections spun by the ruinous course of a modernist utopia that was as destructive as it was unrealistic at the sunset of the postwar boom.

Postmodernism was a fearful escape into an idealized past, whereas Second Century Modernism is distinctly current and provocatively varied. As a conceptually committed vessel for an architecture of action, the forms' corollary to such philosophy remains as diverse as the individual designers that produce them. As an overarching umbrella term, Second Century Modernism is comprehensive of the hyper-technological and the vernacular, without favoring one or the other. It is both the intent and the historical awareness of the design producer and their patron that ultimately stake out the boundaries for the qualitative outcome of any project. The differences between postmodernism and Second Century Modernism are more numerous than any prevision.

Ludwig Hilberseimer, Highrise City, 1926

“Second Century Modernism is filled with aspirations while being grounded in the practical. It is a plea to adopt the emotional richness of past and future architecture without thoughtlessly borrowing its forms”

The Balancing Act

This new century of modernism incorporates a widely diverse input to arrive at the success of the architecture of the past without the stylistic traps. From that perspective, architecture becomes a matter of integration rather than compromise. A coherent, open-ended, directional course of action expresses the vibrancy of this epoch in its constant mutation. Only a few saw in diversity a platform for richness, instead of contamination of a design message. Robert Venturi and Denise Scott Brown made a case for the vernacular to be rehabilitated into the pantheon of design languages, and with that they withdrew from architects any cultural prerogative to design the environment. Second Century Modernism gives that prerogative back to the architect. Bernard Rudofsky brought to the attention of the general public that an architecture without a signature has powerful import in the annals of architecture.

Can this gap be bridged by combining design in its most convincing expressions within a much wider range to create a vibrant vernacular? On the other end of the spectrum is Frank Gehry’s statement that “98% of everything that is built and designed today is pure shit. There is no sense of design, no respect for humanity or for anything else. They are damn buildings and that’s it.”[1] Second Century Modernism is a platform for the 98% by offering a wider arsenal of design options that are naturally more inclusive.

Architecture was, is, and will always be a balancing act. The ability of architects to attend to as many demands placed on the project they are entrusted to design as they can is what makes a difference in the relevance of that piece of architecture in people’s lives. Architecture is both the background of human activity and foreground to the history of that very activity to posterity—a silent testimony over time of the efforts, aspirations, and culture of those who endeavored to build it. Simplifying this ambitious program through trendy shortcuts or misunderstanding of genuine philosophical underpinning misses the underlying mandate of architecture to function at all levels—logistical and symbolic.

Second Century Modernism is filled with aspirations while being grounded in the practical. It is a plea to adopt the emotional richness of past and future architecture without thoughtlessly borrowing its forms. Second Century Modernism puts into question the exclusionary approach to forms and styles. Fortified with the awareness of what was apprehended in the crisis of late modernism, this new time engenders a theater for resonant design that will be based on finding a dynamic balance point within complex systems to create an optimal outcome that is rich, vibrant, and engaging. Digital technology, connectivity, and communication are at the center of this larger paradigm shift in modern life. Architects are in the position to recast their own role in this new trajectory and make lasting built commentaries in the public realm. By linking to global trends while committing to the local, Second Century Modernism’s dual dimension delivers a new way of being in the world.

Modernism is getting a new 100-year lease. This expanded notion of modernism impels cultural vibrancy, emotional meaning, and community engagement as three quintessential goals of a design for tomorrow—all with the hope that this will invite the public to fall in love with architecture once again.

Collaborative writing by John Jennifer Marx and Pierluigi Serraino

[1] https://www.theguardian.com/artanddesign/2014/oct/24/frank-gehry-journalist-finger-architecture-shit

PARADOXEMBRACING

In the West we tend to look at a paradox as a condition to resolve. It feels easier to resort to the binary oppositions that pervade the structures with which we are taught to think, with issues defined in black and white, and hard lines between good and evil, wisdom and ignorance, dominance and supplication. Lost in this approach are the abundant gradations of life that make humanity interesting; lost are the connections between people and things that exist in overlapping boundaries. We might instead consider embracing paradox.

Embracing paradox is about embracing plurality. When confronted with opposing elements that appear to be mutually exclusive, embracing paradox means developing the capacity to conceptualize and, most importantly, *feel* that they can be taken together holistically. It's a matter of simultaneity and balance, and of assessing whether that balance is healthy or hurtful. There is potential here to undo some of the binary thinking that operates across culture, that may be—but is not always—gendered: binaries between the rational and the emotional, between strong and soft, between thinking and caring. Across all these oppositions, I advocate for the beauty and vibrancy in being both.

Particularly intimate and therefore especially significant among these dueling dynamics is the interplay between the heart and the mind. In the context of architectural design, we might look at this as a split between a thought process that is linear, logical, verbal, and ultimately *pragmatic*, and a creative process that is nonlinear, visual, intuitive, and ultimately *emotional*. In professional contexts, even in supposedly creative pursuits, pragmatism is overwhelmingly favored over processes that might be more closely associated with emotionality. Even though we all feel deeply, emotionality has come to be fundamentally connected to social ideas of femininity, thereby trivialized, considered effete and superfluous, and denigrated according to a patriarchal paradigm. But what happens to our professional cultures, to our creative output, to our ways of being in the world, when the emotional is suppressed?

Taken to an extreme, lack of empathy begets cruelty, and when emotionality is disallowed from healthy expression, it can erupt in disastrous ways. Pervasive is the sense of diminished empathy that is so critical to business

“If we are to find a way to embrace this paradox between self-expression and belonging, we will need to celebrate our differences at the same level as we currently cling to conformity”

practices, in which only the cold logic of shareholder value can be legally considered in corporate decision-making in the United States. This transactional logic of economic self-interest will never create a sustaining sense of care or community, nor—in design practices—will it create an environment to develop architectures that are well-loved or that adequately sustain the lives of their inhabitants.

By exploring the paradox dynamic between collaboration and vision, we can seek hybrid models for practice that combine individualistic creative expression with structures that give voice to a greater number and divest from practices that support the fiction of the heroic sole author. Going further, the question remains of how we can use care and emotionality as part of the design process, to blend together the rational and the emotional and design both from the heart and the mind. How would we go about this, and what kinds of architectures could flourish as a result?

There is certainly more that we can accomplish when it comes to developing emotional meaning in our buildings and cities. In 1966, when Robert Venturi wrote, “I like complexity and contradiction in architecture,” he nudged open the door to a vast universe of potential design expression that had been excluded by the “puritanically moral language of orthodox Modern architecture.”[1] These austere and minimalistic architectures of modernism have, over the past century, been heavily revered for their poetry and their power. In an effort to find the essence of architecture, however, modernism has tended to follow a reductivist approach, which, in cases where the pursuit of purity has fallen short of poetry, has had the effect of stripping the architecture of its emotional content. Venturi’s rallying cry to embrace a messy hybrid, of valuing “richness of meaning rather than clarity of meaning” invited us to question rigidity, but it still favored the intellectual over the emotional: as quickly as he supports complexity and contradiction, he also disparages “the precious intricacies of picturesqueness or expressionism.”[2]

Venturi’s attitude is exemplary of the way in which a whole range of creative expressions and aesthetic gestures have been left out of architectural design. In many ways modernism was itself a reaction to the “picturesqueness or expressionism” of earlier styles, and in retaining this point of view, Venturi also left

[1] Robert Venturi, *Complexity and Contradiction in Architecture*, 2nd ed. (New York: The Museum of Modern Art, 1977), 16.

[2] Venturi, *Complexity and Contradiction in Architecture*, 16.

the door half closed to substantive change, deepening the exclusion of emotional meaning as a value in architecture.

The language used to value and describe architecture is significant. Nowhere in *Complexity and Contradiction* does Venturi use the word "beauty." The same year as that book was published, the Temptations recorded the hit single "Beauty Is Only Skin Deep," and American culture was swept up in a transformation of how we see our inner selves in relation to the outside world. Beauty came to be understood as fundamentally superficial and lacking seriousness, with architects reducing the "prettiness" of their designs to be taken with more gravity and refusing to accept that emotional meaning has any value at all.

But could we consider that the proverb "beauty is more than skin deep" might be worthy of our attention? We do, after all, need and want beauty in our lives: emotional resonance forms the basis of human relationships with one another, and is vital to our well-being. Furthermore, the disconnection many feel with their buildings and cities only contributes to ambivalence about their preservation, where much is needlessly demolished and rebuilt at great cost to the environment. Considering that the most sustainable things in life might be those you will never throw away because you love them too much, emotional meaning might play a vital role in building sustainably. Without an emotional engagement with buildings and cities that are beautiful, lovable, and *demanding* of care, we will continue to destroy our surroundings, haunting modern life and damaging the planet.

Let us consider other paradox dynamics: between alienation and vibrancy, globalization and individual expression. Different architectures might provoke different emotional responses in different people, and beauty and lovability can be seen as highly subjective. How might we design in a way that will be emotionally resonant right across a range of cultural and individual contexts, without slipping into genericism? What might be helpful is to look at lovable design not as a specific style, but as more of a set of emotional intentions. How do we want people to feel about the space, what emotions are appropriate for the project to be successful? Welcoming, hopeful, comforting, uplifting, humane, and optimistic are all emotions that are often overlooked or abstracted past a point of resonance. To create architectures that are resonant and welcoming and well-loved, that support the full range of human expression, we need those architectures to *themselves* have a sense of humanity, and of individual expression.

"Lovability" might best be approached broadly as a set of intentions rather than as an issue of style. That is to say, one might start with a set of intentions to create "lovable design" and to look at that question deeply, from a perspective of emotional meaning and resonance. One can then search for a formal expression of those intentions that fits the context, client, building use, and artistic interests of the project designer and team. Rather than assigning a specific "style" to be the lovable one, it might be better to encourage the widest possible range for self-expression.

There is a fundamental reciprocity here, between the individual and their environment, where more loving and emotionally resonant buildings and cities will support a public that is more loving and emotionally responsive, and vice versa. What we, as humans, seem to universally seek is the opportunity to sing with a clear and resounding voice—a voice of self-determination which cannot be imposed upon or constrained by others. At the same time, we want to have that voice accepted and supported by the communities that surround us. If we are to find a way to embrace this paradox between self-expression and belonging, we will need to celebrate our differences at the same level as we currently cling to conformity.

We are in the midst of a compelling evolution, if not revolution, but it takes time for humans to adapt to change. There is an incredible opportunity to explore the rich emotional landscape that has gone unheard. There is a powerful sense of insight that comes from being in the in-between spaces of a largely binary culture. From conflict we can emerge with new perspectives, as it is often the differences between us that creates the conditions for humanity to thrive. Let us aspire to unlock the resplendent feast that our emotionally rich, diverse, and holistic world can provide if we listen with intention.

As we take a step

out into the world, each morning
we are confronted by a balance dynamic
with the world.
If we are lucky,
it is an existential dynamic,
rather than a material survival equation.
There is a moment,
in the lives of most artists,
where we see that we exist in relationship
to a complex world—a world of paradox,
of abundance and scarcity, of pleasure and pain,
of epic beauty and inexplicable tragedy.
At some point we might realize
that the world can be absurd and often unfair.
In some measure
we have to define our relationship
to this newfound sense
of the world
in our mind and
in our heart.

For some people,
this means taking a reactionary approach
to gather resources, primarily for the
self-preservation and protection of
your internal world.
For others, for me, this means taking a
reflective approach, to marshal
what abundance life gives you in order
to create positive change
in the external
world.

For me
this epiphany
occurred
when I
was quite
young.

My first love
was for drawing,
then painting,
both mediums
for the creation of imaginary worlds.
In the Midwest, where I grew up,
these were not considered suitable endeavors
for making a living,
and so, architecture became my chosen focus.
I assumed it was a creative profession
that could provide an outlet for this intense passion.
Later, when I had become a young architect,
I realized that while architecture does indeed
have a creative mission,
it carries a heavy pragmatic burden.
There are long stretches
where architecture could not sustain the need
for artistic expression.
This is due to the drawn-out nature of
the "idea to finished building" cycle,
as buildings can take years to construct.
Throughout my adult life I have turned to
painting, drawing, photography, and poetry
to fulfill this need.
At first this took the form of
almost pure self-expression,
a reflection on what moved me,
of a search for meaning,
it was self-referential and,
in a sense,
self-satisfying.

My artistic intention
involves expressing complex ideas
thru a highly emotional format,
where cleverness is not required to understand
the most fundamental aspects of the work.
Here intellectual concepts
are layered on top of the emotional
experience,
this enhances the experience,
but takes an "in addition to" approach,
in that the various intellectual overlays
enhance the primary content,
but are not essential.
The work embraces ambiguity,
thus leaving itself open
to interpretation.

VISUAL LECTURE

HOW SHOULD I SPEAK?

Epiphanies can be a powerful force,
when embraced with passion

Within this awareness
a fundamental question becomes ...
how, in practice, should one respond to the human condition?

As an artist this might take many broad forms
in sharing your humanity .....
in advocating for change
in participating in change

In my particular case, I found two paths:

One way is to draw, to create, to build
this has been my body of work as an architectural designer
to give form to concepts that respond to the spirit of the times

Another way is to speak, and to write
this took a bit of courage to step
outside of the safety of a quiet practice
to put ideas forward .....
to learn to write in compelling prose

In 2015, we redesigned our website at Form4. As part of this effort, I felt the need to visually describe an architectural design philosophy that would combine my background as a painter with my skills as a poet. This led to exploring a variation on a new genre in the arts called the "Visual Poem."

To craft this idea at the highest possible level the project became a deep collaboration between graphic artist Jeremy Mende, architectural writer Pierluigi Serraino, and myself. We created 12 visual poems and narratives for a collateral event at the 2016 Venice Architecture Biennale.

In 2018, with the publication of *The Absurdity of Beauty*, I used those Visual Poems, now grown to a total collection of 18, to explain the concepts behind the book in a lecture format.

The initial lecture occurred in 2019 at the AIA San Francisco and consisted of 98 slides. Over the years, this lecture has been given in multiple venues around the world and has expanded to 167 slides. Offered here is a condensed version, true to the spirit of the original Visual Poems, minimalist in format, inviting the viewer to engage in exploring a multiplicity of meaning and the open-ended potential to draw alternative conclusions.

Dynamic Balance

We all exist in a Balance Dynamic with the world

We asked ourselves:

When did the world become so gray?
When did the public fall out of love with the built environment?
When did our profession polarize so deeply between the pragmatic and the self-indulgent?
When did we begin to neglect the people we pledged to care for?

We could debate the causal merits of modernism in this disconnection,
the difficulty in translating a minimalist approach to a wider culture.
Have we exhausted the conceit yet "that the public just needs to catch up"?

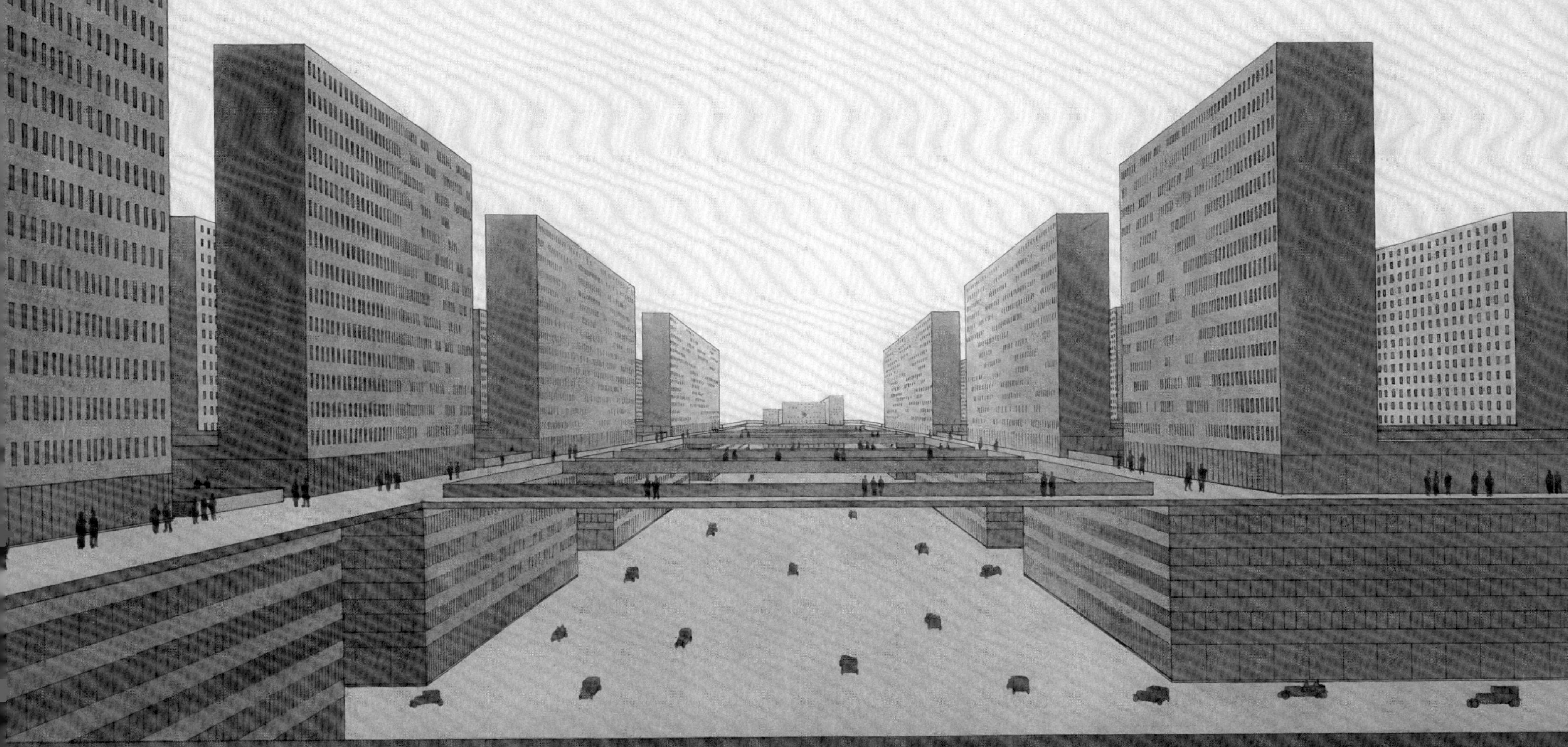

DISCONNECTED

Forbes

Architecture Continues To Implode: More Insiders Admit The Profession Is Failing

Frank Gehry Is Right: 98% Of Architecture Today 'Has No Respect For Humanity'

Is our cultural media's obsession with "Starchitecture" the real issue we should address?

This is the architecture we live with,
the 80%, the ordinary ...

One of the worst reactions to the banality of modern design is to fall back to historicism

"A Plea for Beauty: A Manifesto for a New Urbanism" by Roger Scruton

In 2019, the Trump administration floated an idea of requiring all federal buildings to be designed in a neoclassical style

Bloomberg–Harris Poll 2020 > 72% of Americans chose historicist architecture over modernism

Even in our allied field of the arts, we find a perceived binary paradox between architecture and humanity

ANIMA ANIMUS

Above: Maria Kochetkova and Joseph Walsh rehearsing Dawson's Anima Animus // © Erik Tomasson. Head shot: David Dawson // © Patrick Wamsganz

Anima Animus offers a rich mix of contrasts, most meaningful among them Carl Jung's concept of animus (the male aspect of the female psyche) and anima (the female aspect of the male psyche). Another contrast can be found in the music by Italian composer Ezio Bosso. "It felt to me like music that looks to the past and the future at the same time, much how I like to make dance," Dawson says.

In making this ballet, Dawson found himself responding to the polarized present-day world. He understands the world's opposites—light and dark, humanity and architecture, individual and group—"but between those opposites, there's so much room where people can have choice without judgment," he says. The spaces between extremes are a kind of fluidity, which Dawson wanted to explore within dance. "My language is the classical art form; I'm trying to do something with that," he says. Historically, some ballet steps are for women or men only; Dawson shifts this by giving "the opposing energy as a starting point"—in other words, giving animus choreography to a dancer who seems more anima, and vice versa. At times he gives the same choreography to both genders; for example, Principal Dancer Carlo Di Lanno's solo starts with some of the movement from Principal Dancer Maria Kochetkova's solo, then goes in a different direction. In the "Angels" part of the second movement, "we go to archetype," Dawson says. "In Jung's philosophy, the female is the nurturer, the mother, the angel, the pure. And the man is the warrior, the strong, the hero. I'm trying to show it all." Even in these archetypes, the theme of contrasts shows—the two principal women, Kochetkova and Principal Dancer Sofiane Sylve, couldn't be more different. Watching them do the same steps, you see the potential in the movement—there is never only one way. Then, when the women float high above

Anima Animus offers a rich mix of contrasts, most meaningful among them Carl Jung's concept of animus (the male aspect of the female psyche) and anima (the female aspect of the male psyche). Another contrast can be found in the music by Italian composer Ezio Bosso. "It felt to me like music that looks to the past and the future at the same time, much how I like to make dance," Dawson says.

In making this ballet, Dawson found himself responding to the polarized present-day world. He understands the world's opposites—light and dark, humanity and architecture, individual and group—"but between those opposites, there's so much room where people can have choice without judgment," he says. The spaces between extremes are a kind of fluidity, which Dawson wanted to explore within dance. "My language is the classical art form; I'm trying to do something with that," he says. Historically, some ballet steps are for women or men only; Dawson shifts this by giving "the opposing energy as a starting point"—in other words, giving animus choreography to a

Why can't we have both?

THIS

IS WHAT I FEAR MOST

Banality can exist in developing as well as rich countries; relentless boxes that are unlovable

Mumbai, India

The Gold Coast, Chicago, USA

Where does this come from?

Venturi + Scott Brown

Postmodernism

The Last 50 Years

Beauty is Only Skin Deep

Poetic (Minimalism)

Innovation

A Short Personal (somewhat simplistic) History

Learning from Las Vegas
Complexity and Contradiction in Architecture

Robert Venturi and Denise Scott Brown

Less is More ...

Mies van der Rohe

Less is a Bore ...

Robert Venturi and Denise Scott Brown

Less + More ...

John Marx

Postmodernism

We have been here before ...

The Dalí Theater-Museum, Figueres, Spain, designed by Salvador Dalí

Prior to the mid-1960s, common and architectural culture embraced beauty

Postmodernism brought the awkward scale of a cartoon

Architects have not been allowed to design

beautiful buildings

in the last 50 years

In 1966, two things contributed to change that notion

1

"Beauty is Only Skin Deep" (The Temptations)

2

Robert Venturi negated the arbitrary aspects of beauty in *Complexity and Contradiction*

Broadly architectural culture moved away from the subjective nature of emotions in favor of the efficiency and efficacy of logic and reason. The profession of architecture and fine arts institutions reinterpreted this to mean anything that was beautiful was superficial.

Beauty is more than Skin Deep
Beauty is in the Eye of the Beholder

Descartes 1635
I think
therefore I am
I care
therefore we are
John Jennifer Marx 2024
MIND
A QUARTERLY REVIEW
OF
PSYCHOLOGY AND PHILOSOPHY

To be considered arbitrary is perhaps the greatest sin of all

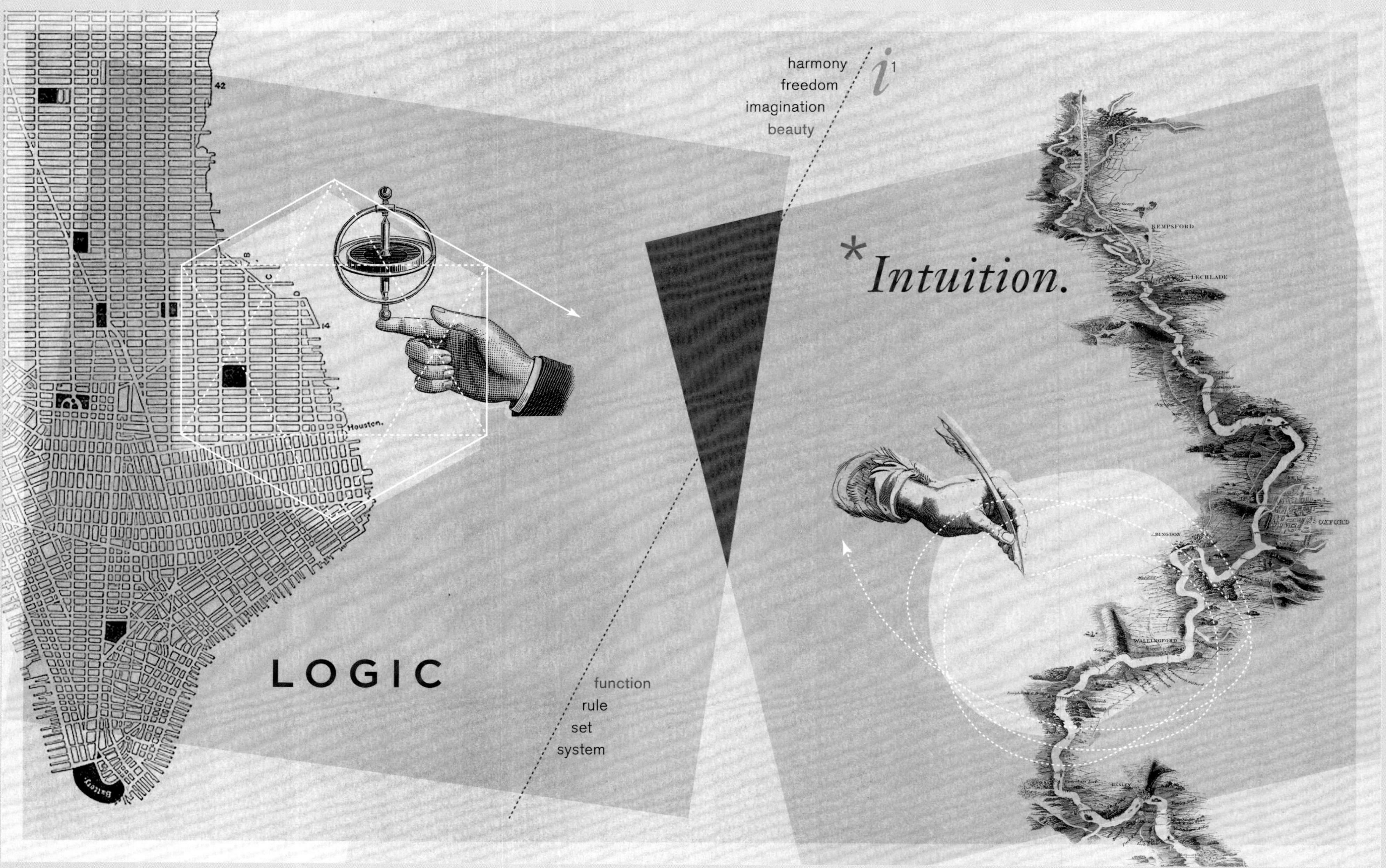

Linear + Logical + Verbal

Nonlinear + Intuitive + Visual

A Balance Equation

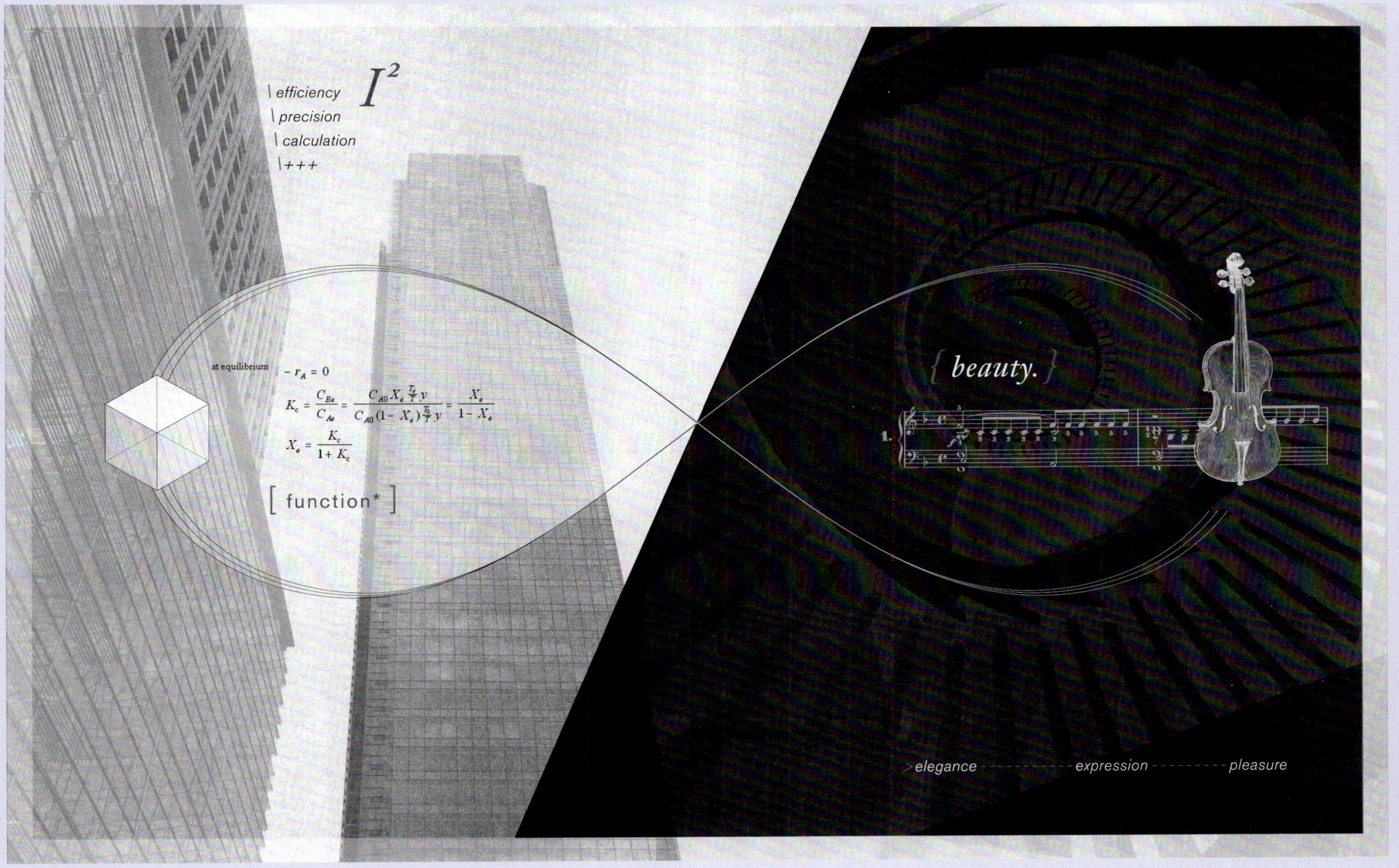

\ efficiency
\ precision
\ calculation
\ +++

I^2

at equilibrium

$$-r_A = 0$$

$$K_c = \frac{C_{Be}}{C_{Ae}} = \frac{C_{A0} X_e \frac{T_0}{T} y}{C_{A0}(1 - X_e)\frac{T_0}{T} y} = \frac{X_e}{1 - X_e}$$

$$X_e = \frac{K_c}{1 + K_c}$$

[function*]

{ beauty. }

> elegance ---------- expression ---------- pleasure

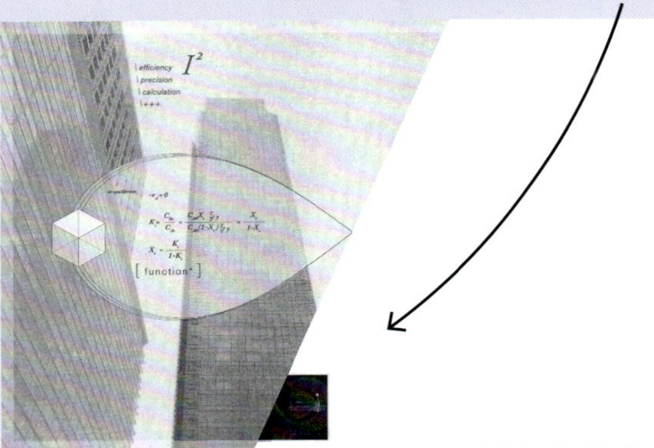

The architectural profession tends to follow this proportion

How do we balance emotion into our design process?

The most sustainable things in life are those things that you won't throw away because you love them too much.

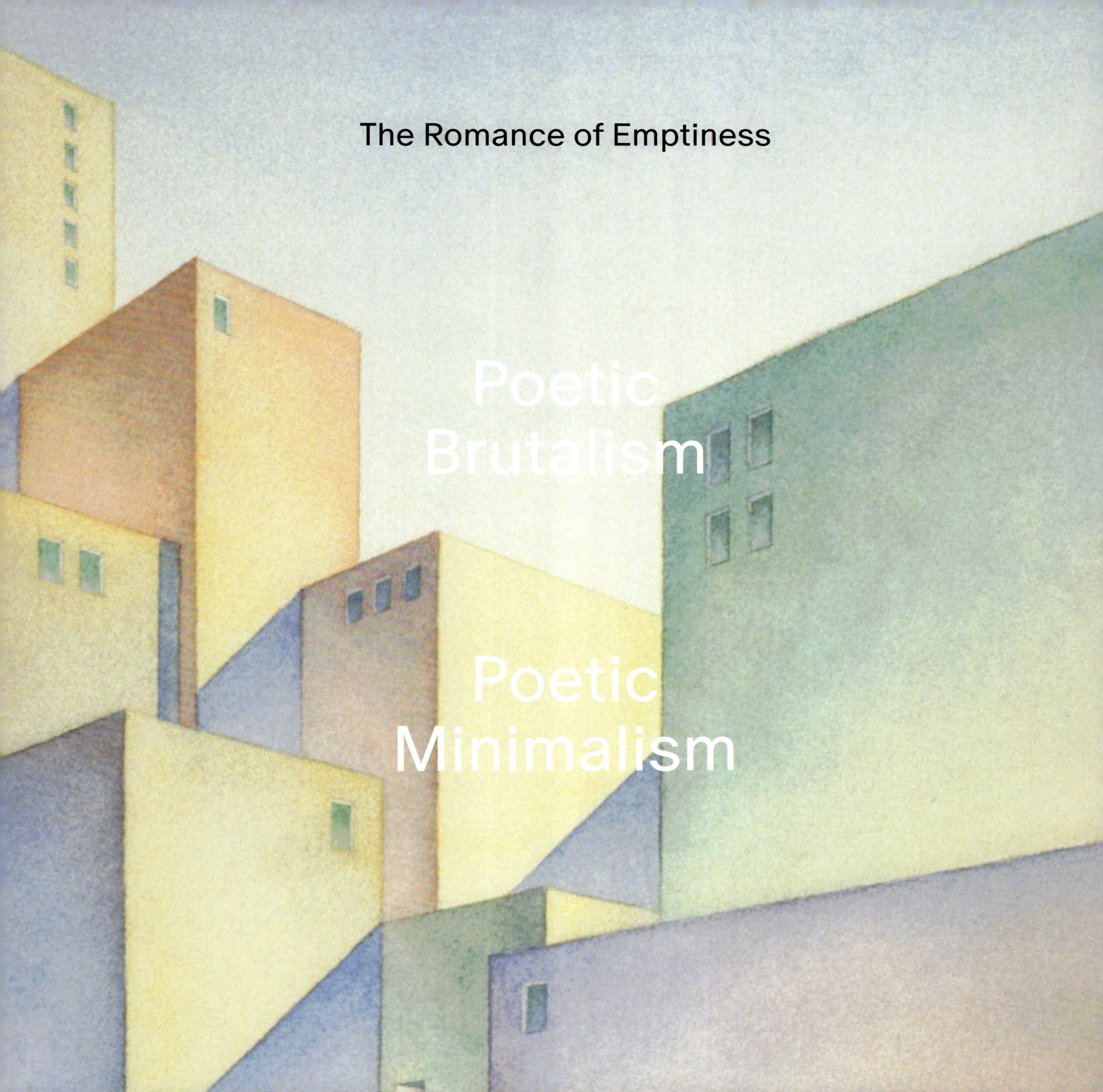
The Romance of Emptiness
Poetic
Brutalism
Poetic
Minimalism

This building by Renzo Piano directly and beautifully relates to the powerfully poetic forms found in historic Malta and in the landscape.

Poetic Brutalism

Louis Kahn
The Salk Institute
La Jolla, CA

The Emptiness of Minimalism

I challenge the notion of a “Reductivist Approach,”
the banality of minimist glass, the relentless emptiness of articulated “neobrutalism.”

Brutalism at the Barbican

Why not just Poetic?

There is a common aspiration towards “Invisible Architecture.” “We are the frame, not the picture”
Background does not mean banal.
Design should add to the cultural fabric.

The Curious Nature of the "Cult of Innovation"

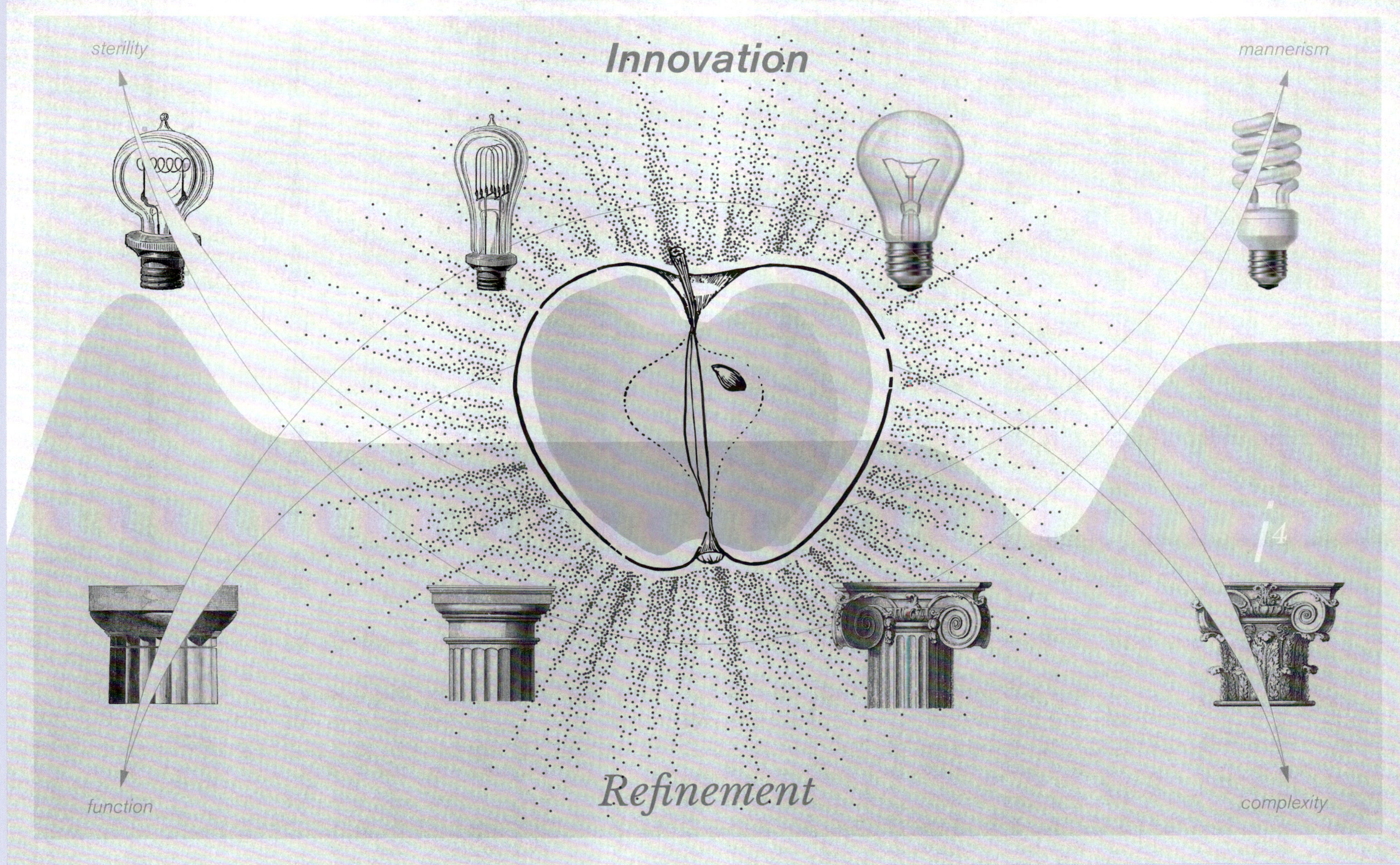

It took 2,500 years to go from a crude Greek Doric column to Palladio's perfect Tuscan column. Innovation and refinement take time.

Emotional Meaning

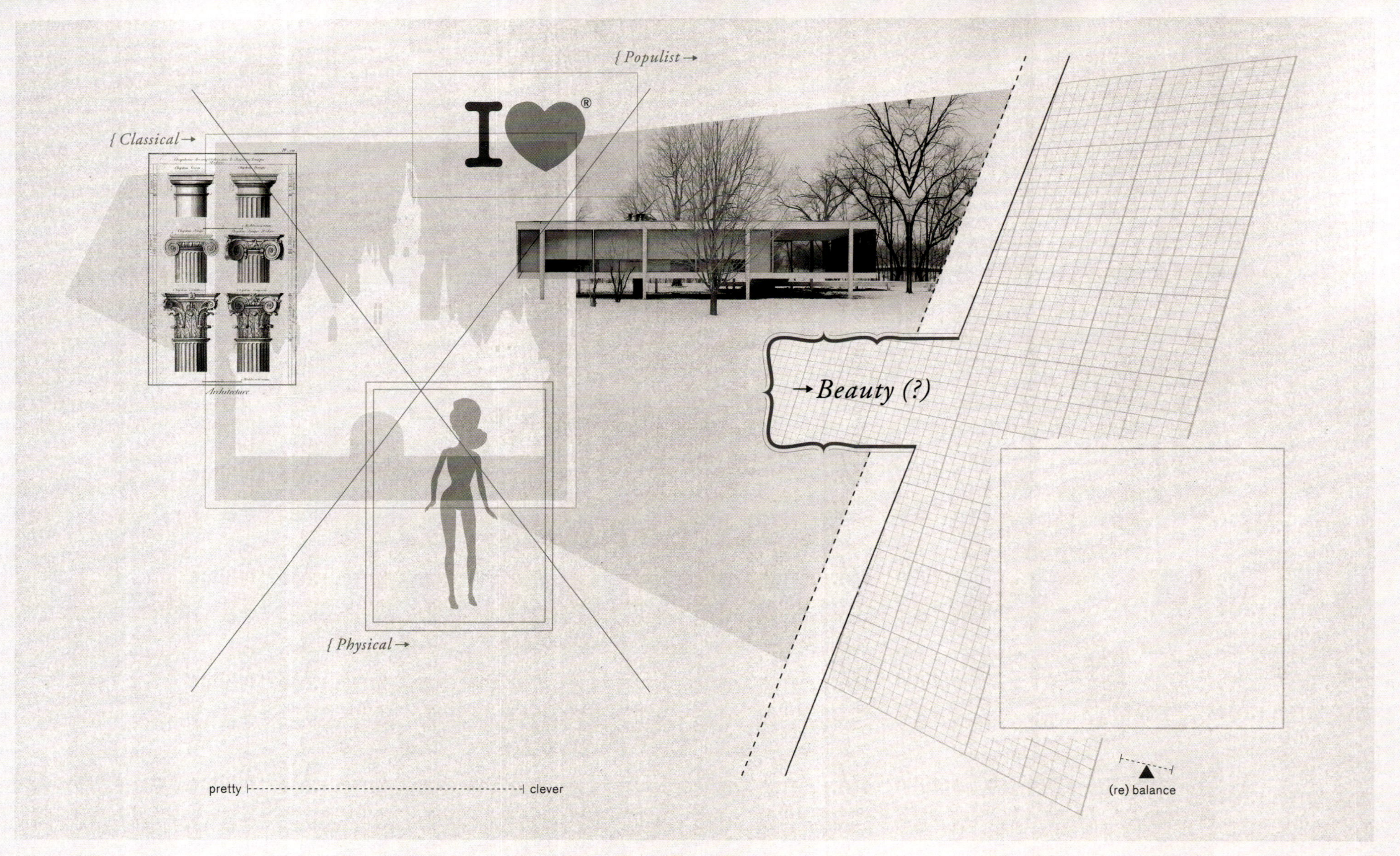

Five issues to address: Nostalgia, Commercialism, Iconicity, Superficiality, Authenticity

The Changing Potential of Architecture A Dynamic Chart

Classification is an ancient craft to help humanity understand and navigate the world we inhabit. The following chart is as ambitious as it is operational in the attempt to comprehend the intersection of the paths between modernity and architecture.

Temporal categories are outlined in four columns: Historicism, Modernism, Present Day, and Second Century Modernism. These represent time blocks of uneven duration. It is a suggested time sequence based on a personal reading of perceived large-scale facts and their interrelationship to a likely design outcome. These four headings map the chronology of the open-ended list of categories across the century, highlighting how ongoing concerns of architectural culture find renewed forms under changing conditions. The first three columns represent an analysis of where we have progressed from, while the fourth column offers a vision of the future (hence Second Century Modernism), a possible configuration of things to come in the realm of architecture.

Counterpoint to these vertical historical slices are five horizontal categories that together create a dynamic matrix in motion. In one way or another all designs come to terms with this cluster. Architecture manifests itself in a particular Form, embodying a Concept, engaging specific Technologies, producing in the user an Emotion largely determined by Cultural circumstances. This is an ahistorical condition that can be traced under any circumstances, ages, and latitudes. Over time, these five rows have changed their importance factor in the design community. Concept and Technology loom large today while emotional meaning and culture have become much smaller. This in many ways illustrates our current condition of alienation in relationship to the public, and their lack of affection for Modernism. Each row is further broken down with lines depicting changes in value using verbal descriptors. At times these changes swing back and forth in a dialectic fashion as ideas have reached their apex of value and in their inevitable decline have produced counterreactions in the design culture. In the past, the lines between these categories have been sharply drawn. However, in Second Century Modernism, the rows are seen to coexist in a state of dynamic balance; in fact, they are ultimately portrayed as overlaying each other, enriching each other, synergistically enhancing their effectiveness and meaning.

In this humanity graph we come with a point of view. We delve into an investigative endeavor to draw imaginary lines between floating dots in the fuzzy vision of where the here and now is, and towards a future—fundamentally to shed clarity, in one image, on all that makes us what we are.

We invite a dialogue for others to suggest alternatives to this condition.

Temptations Toward Abundance

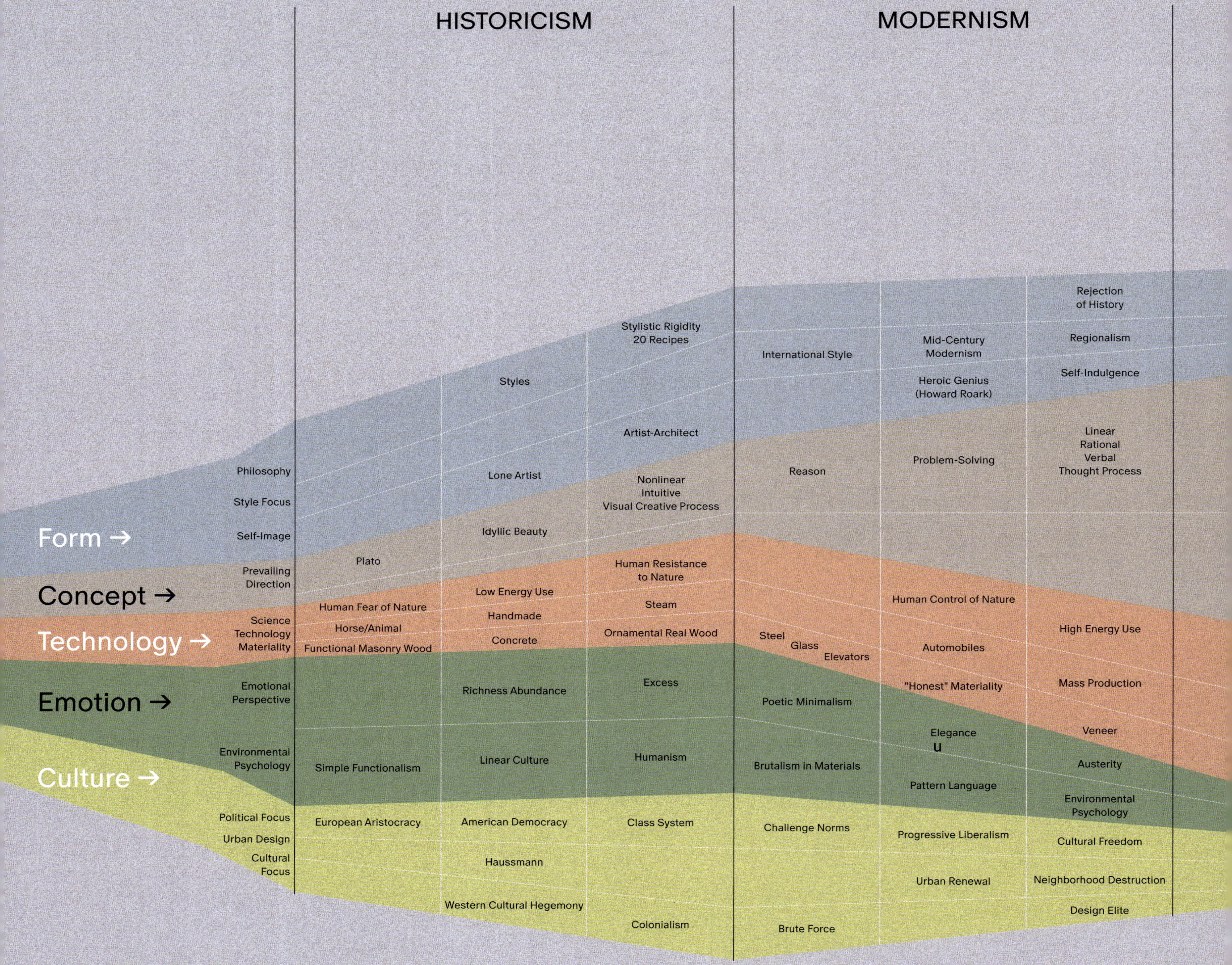

HISTORICISM

MODERNISM

Form →

Concept →

Technology →

Emotion →

Culture →

Philosophy
Style Focus
Self-Image
Prevailing Direction
Science
Technology
Materiality
Emotional Perspective
Environmental Psychology
Political Focus
Urban Design
Cultural Focus

Plato
Human Fear of Nature
Horse/Animal
Functional Masonry Wood
Simple Functionalism
European Aristocracy

Styles
Lone Artist
Idyllic Beauty
Low Energy Use
Handmade
Concrete
Richness Abundance
Linear Culture
American Democracy
Haussmann
Western Cultural Hegemony

Stylistic Rigidity
20 Recipes
Artist-Architect
Nonlinear
Intuitive
Visual Creative Process
Human Resistance to Nature
Steam
Ornamental Real Wood
Excess
Humanism
Class System
Colonialism

International Style
Reason
Steel
Glass
Elevators
Poetic Minimalism
Brutalism in Materials
Challenge Norms
Brute Force

Mid-Century Modernism
Heroic Genius (Howard Roark)
Problem-Solving
Human Control of Nature
Automobiles
"Honest" Materiality
Elegance
Pattern Language
Progressive Liberalism
Urban Renewal

Rejection of History
Regionalism
Self-Indulgence
Linear
Rational
Verbal
Thought Process
High Energy Use
Mass Production
Veneer
Austerity
Environmental Psychology
Cultural Freedom
Neighborhood Destruction
Design Elite

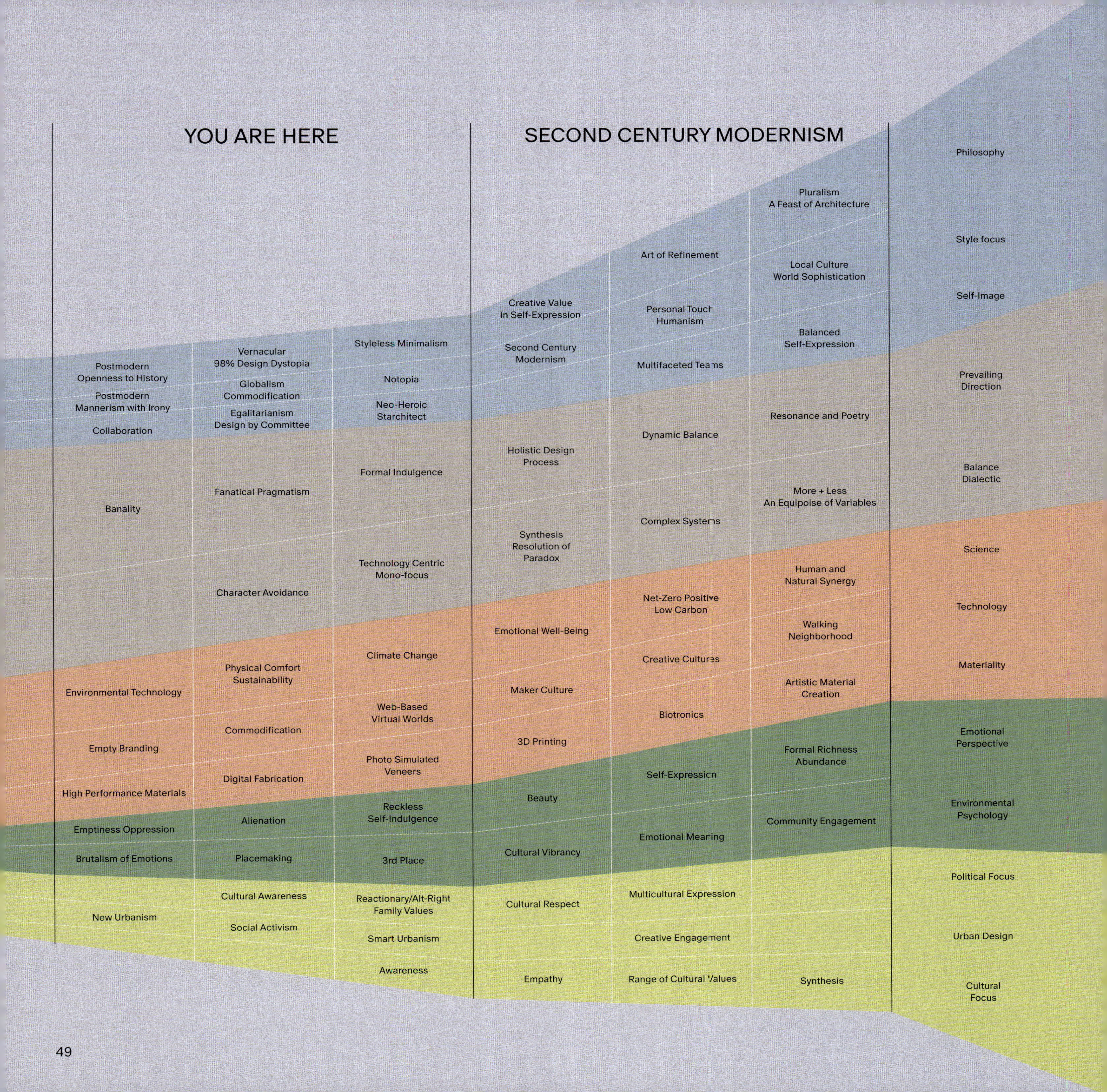

YOU ARE HERE

Postmodern
Openness to History

Postmodern
Mannerism with Irony

Collaboration

Banality

Environmental Technology

Empty Branding

High Performance Materials

Emptiness Oppression

Brutalism of Emotions

New Urbanism

Vernacular
98% Design Dystopia

Globalism
Commodification

Egalitarianism
Design by Committee

Fanatical Pragmatism

Character Avoidance

Physical Comfort
Sustainability

Commodification

Digital Fabrication

Alienation

Placemaking

Cultural Awareness

Social Activism

Styleless Minimalism

Notopia

Neo-Heroic
Starchitect

Formal Indulgence

Technology Centric
Mono-focus

Climate Change

Web-Based
Virtual Worlds

Photo Simulated
Veneers

Reckless
Self-Indulgence

3rd Place

Reactionary/Alt-Right
Family Values

Smart Urbanism

Awareness

SECOND CENTURY MODERNISM

Creative Value
in Self-Expression

Second Century
Modernism

Holistic Design
Process

Synthesis
Resolution of
Paradox

Emotional Well-Being

Maker Culture

3D Printing

Beauty

Cultural Vibrancy

Cultural Respect

Empathy

Art of Refinement

Personal Touch
Humanism

Multifaceted Teams

Dynamic Balance

Complex Systems

Net-Zero Positive
Low Carbon

Creative Cultures

Biotronics

Self-Expression

Emotional Meaning

Multicultural Expression

Creative Engagement

Range of Cultural Values

Pluralism
A Feast of Architecture

Local Culture
World Sophistication

Balanced
Self-Expression

Resonance and Poetry

More + Less
An Equipoise of Variables

Human and
Natural Synergy

Walking
Neighborhood

Artistic Material
Creation

Formal Richness
Abundance

Community Engagement

Synthesis

Philosophy

Style focus

Self-Image

Prevailing
Direction

Balance
Dialectic

Science

Technology

Materiality

Emotional
Perspective

Environmental
Psychology

Political Focus

Urban Design

Cultural
Focus

Range of Cultural Inclusion

As a profession, we live in an insular bubble, but we should embrace the world of vibrant humanity that lies outside.

Creating vibrancy in odd and unexpected ways

Tourist Vibrancy

Urban Vibrancy

Signs of Life

Sea Monsters HERE, Filthy Luker + Pedro Estrellas

Challenging Norms, Embracing Paradox

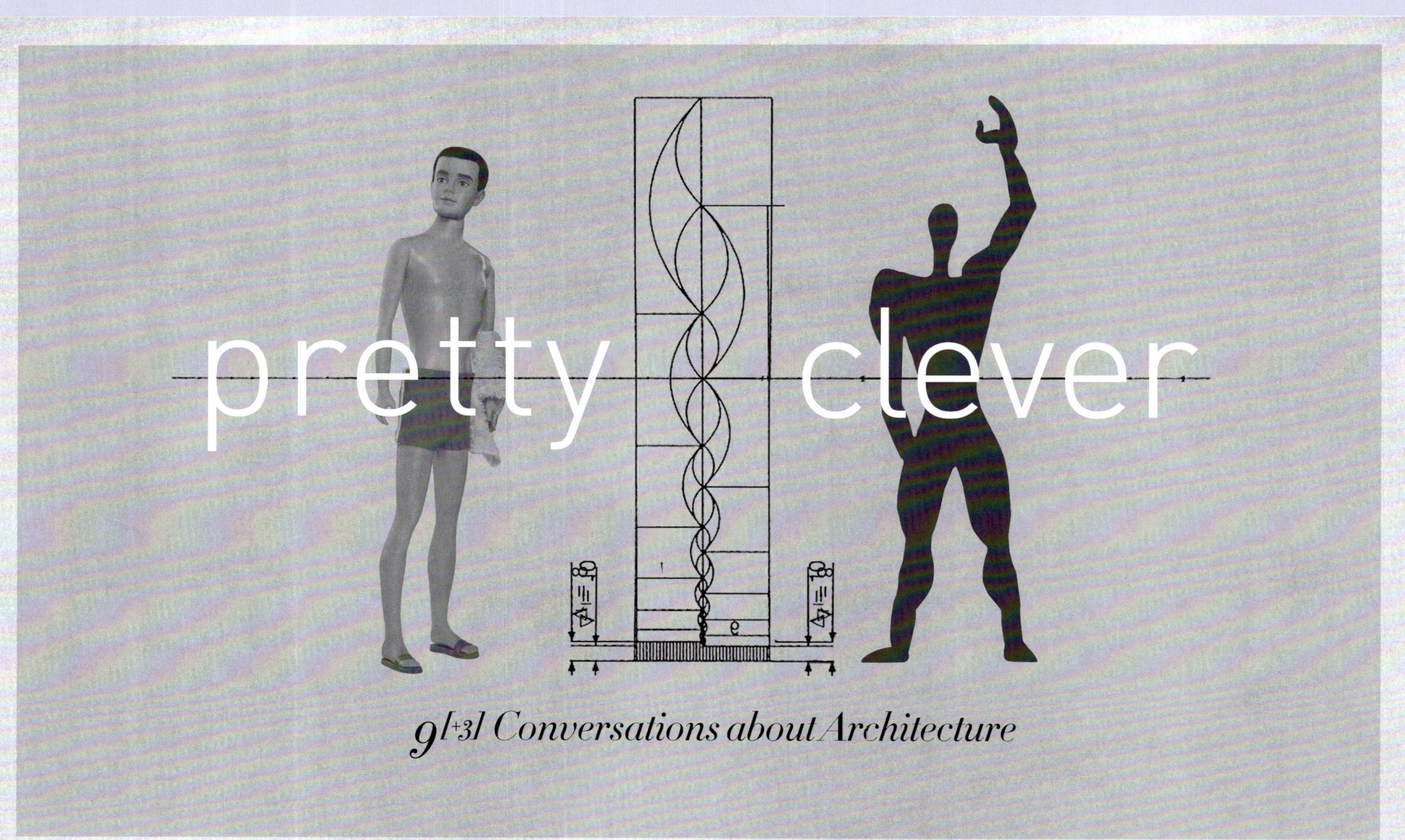

Celebrating the complex feast of architecture

We can enjoy everything on the banquet table.

Three Questions:

Question 1:
Why should we love this design?

Question 2:
What emotions does this building evoke?

Question 3:
Does this design promote "An Architecture of Emotional Abundance"?

All buildings create Emotional Meaning:

Hopeful	Welcoming	Optimistic
Oppressive	Depressing	Heavy

Have you loved a building today?

POEM 3

A young high school girl
aspiring to become an architect
sits in a large hall
filled with an excited audience of designers

it's quite an honor for this modest coastal city
to have a speaker of such stature
unveiling a design for their city hall

she sits with her aunt's friend
an architect
for 20 years
she has
enjoyed the graces
of a creative profession
of health insurance,
a 401k plan, and
paid maternity leave

she has also
sustained a burden
that comes with the awkward balancing
of art and business

The architect ascends the podium
to enthusiastic applause
he is part of the 2% of the profession
that has built a critical practice
that has an agency
that comes from the credibility of fame

he speaks
with the eloquent voice of a poet
of how beautifully
the soft light
will caress the raw concrete

of how the shadows will
create a vibrancy of textural delight
of how he has reduced
everything to its true essence
he speaks
of the beauty
and care
and thoughtfulness of the design
he speaks
of grand ideas
of concepts
that were the foundations of his design
he reveals
how the long monolithic nature
of the parti will inspire learning
and community engagement
He speaks from a heart
full of passion
and with a warm dignity
that years of public speaking will help you craft
and when
he is finished with building an anticipation
with a crescendo of alluring words
he reveals the first rendering
compositionally flawless
refined
and understated
to which the audience
well educated in the nuances of
normative minimalism
offers its appreciation
but the young girl
untrained
naively asks her aunt's friend
when is he going to show the building
he just described?
I've fallen in love with his ideas...
his words
sound like sweet music
To which her aunt's friend replies
it's here, sweetheart
austerity of the entry plaza

she explains,
with a kind patience,
how this design fits into the history of architecture
how clever the architect was in this bit of detailing
how the grid reflects a distant relationship
to a building across town

and yet the girl
unmoved...refuses to concede

The building he described
that I imagined...
I can't see that anywhere in these renderings
This building seems cold and empty
there is nothing lovable I can point to

yes, there is a daring cantilever
but that makes me feel a little uneasy
those concrete walls

feel relentless

and oppressive

her mother taught her to boldly think for herself
to question her instincts
but to avoid
feeling undereducated
like there was a vast secret language
she simply needs to learn

Her questions
seemed thoughtful
for one so young

I was hoping for more...
why is there no color
no warmth
no sense of hope

After a long pause...
Her aunt's friend
stated that
architecture is complicated
when you go to architecture school you will understand
they will show you buildings like this
that will make your heart soar
and inspire you
when minimalism hits the right key...
the extraordinary can happen

But,
shouldn't I understand without the training?
Shouldn't a building give me everything I need to fall in love with it?
or is a sense of love not important

he used that word

I wrote it down

I know he has a great deal of experience
and we might differ about concept of the beautiful
but
it feels like he did not make an effort

I tried to find the aspects he spoke of
in the forms he created
the emotions he described
don't seem to have a place in this design

She understands now
how she might make a difference in this mysterious profession
...to match form to the poetry of intention.

EXPRESSIONISM

EXPRESSIONISM

LYRICAL LYRICAL LYRICAL LYRICAL EXPRESSIONISM LYRICAL LYRICAL LYRICAL LYRICAL

LYRICAL LYRICAL LYRICAL EXPRESSIONISM LYRICAL LYRICAL LYRICAL

LYRICAL LYRICAL EXPRESSIONISM LYRICAL LYRICAL

LYRICAL EXPRESSIONISM LYRICAL

LYRICAL EXPRESSIONISM LYRICAL

LYRICAL EXPRESSIONISM LYRICAL

LYRICAL EXPRESSIONISM EXPRESSIONISM LYRICAL

LYRICAL EXPRESSIONISM LYRICAL

LYRICAL EXPRESSIONISM EXPRESSIONISM LYRICAL

LYRICAL EXPRESSIONISM EXPRESSIONISM EXPRESSIONISM LYRICAL

LYRICAL EXPRESSIONISM EXPRESSIONISM EXPRESSIONISM LYRICAL

LYRICAL EXPRESSIONISM EXPRESSIONISM EXPRESSIONISM EXPRESSIONISM EXPRESSIONISM EXPRESSIONISM LYRICAL

Poetry
To aspire toward a condition of poetry in architecture, one might take a series of specific or sometimes seemingly random paths. That movement is both a personal and public commitment to a journey. It begins with the will to listen to the site, the user, the client, absorbing layers of context—cultural, emotive, and physical—with consideration given to the need for efficiency in all things. Inspiration becomes vision; the physical prompts form; the emotive provokes concept. Ideas begin to connect. They coalesce but also diverge, inspiring new directions.

Narrative
Sometimes a narrative emerges, when and if it is strong enough to provide a starting point, a focus, an opportunity to tell a story. It can approach the lyrical. Symbolic constructs start to emerge. Meanings shift and evolve, creating new openings for resonance. It can seem like wandering but with an intention and awareness, inviting considerations of form.

Form
Giving form to ideas is a uniquely human enterprise, paradoxical in a multiplicity of ways. It is a balance of deeply personal inner worlds of the imagination and communal interchanges—the sharing of ideas, fertile with the joys of collaborative exchange.

One of the greater temptations in exploring form and imagery is to experiment with fluidity and the expressive nature of the curve; the drama of which—iconic or not—needs to be thoughtfully calibrated to the context, the program, and the client. The combination of a strong narrative with compelling form lays a foundation for Lyrical Expressionism. When these two resonate, extraordinary things can happen—emotional engagement sparking the mind and heart to moments of clarity. Form requires a commitment to be specific, to build. While forms can hold multiple meanings, they remain one object in concert with others, creating relationships, harmony, and balance.

There are three formal concepts that I have found worth exploring:

Fluidity **Curvaceousness** **Naturalism**

Fluidity
Flow is a common denominator in both ease of use and the lyricism of form. For goods, services, and people all flow. A perception of movement in buildings and cities can provide a sense of energy and dynamism, drawing you in and inviting you to share a journey. Tempting you with mystery and wonder.

Curvaceousness
It is easy as a poet to be drawn toward the curvilinear, the serpentine, the sinuous arc that by its nature charms you. The curve embodies the flow of vitality finding its way into the physical world.

The curve is a powerfully poetic means to express dynamic flow with elegance and intention. This formal relationship can create a cohesiveness between a wide variety of uses and needs, unattainable with the rigidity of the straight line.

In nature, the curve's prevalence is irrepressible whereas the straight line makes a rare appearance. Curves can bend to the aesthetic arc of the universe. Where the sea meets the sky is not a straight line despite a millennium of humans believing so.

Naturalism
A love of nature and natural form is considered a universal constant of the human condition. I have found that the range of manifestations of nature and the possibilities of the organic captivate and inspire me toward formal experimentation. Nature evolves and provokes. The creative tension between the organic and the linear, the natural and the human can reach deeply into our emotions through the lyricism of dynamic form, providing the inspiration to create buildings and cities with kindness, thoughtfulness, and care.

Clarity
When clarity of form pairs with emotional meaning, placemaking follows, communities form, relationships deepen. People become engaged with their environments. In all this, Lyrical Expressionism aspires to create an architecture that straddles both the iconic and the humane.

Intertwined Eternities

A place to meditate, to meander, to mourn, to record, to remember, to recommit. Intertwined Eternities embraces a dynamic between heaven and earth, between life and death, eternal yet unanswerable questions that require a combination of an open mind and a gentle heart.

The architecture of the columbarium approaches these questions in a meaningful way, turning to symbolism as a means to engage the intellect, and heightening the emotional experience to spark the imagination. The role of the architecture here invites the participation of the visitor in a way that asks profound questions, that encourages one to explore, rather than attempting to provide simple answers to complex issues.

A choreographed sequence of open-air stone pavilions, the columbarium reads like a meeting of intertwining outdoor rooms. The weight and sense of permanence offered by its high stone walls contrast with the lightness and ever-changing seasonality of the surrounding landscape framed by picturesque apertures punctuating the walls. Here, architecture and nature exist in state of equipoise.

The interlaced form of the architecture alludes to the immeasurable number of different journeys taken through life by individuals who nevertheless belong to a connected humankind. Six arced segments exist independently while each is interrelated to the others. They can be read as two sinusoidal curves intersecting to create almond-shaped outdoor areas, as well as a labyrinth of stone walls creating a path of discoveries, providing a sense of movement that symbolizes the interconnectedness of all things in life and nature. In marking the ground with their thickness, they convey stability, authority, and timelessness. That width becomes a space of otherworldly inhabitation: hundreds of urns are located here according to a random pattern conferring additional resonance to the texture emerging from the sunlight gracing its ragged stone surfaces. As in a Christian church, the central arch is symbolic of the tomb of Jesus and is positioned at the pinnacle of the main sanctuary for ceremonies and processions.

The design of the columbarium also symbolizes the transition between birth and death, and our inevitable return to Nature. Each wall points to the next, emphasizing the sense of transition through movement. This notion of passage, or flux, is counterbalanced by a strong desire to create a building that is also, in spirit, eternal and fixed. Interpretation of the monumental plays equally with both a sense of gravitas and the idea of the fleeting or ephemeral. The architecture describes both stillness and movement.

Natural light and the surrounding landscape are the quiet companions of an environment where silence plays a big role in feeling this sense of lineage. The fluid geometry accommodates the slow steps of those engaging the memories of their loved ones. These are gentle design gestures meant to hold the living in a metaphorical embrace to soothe their sense of loss, while offering solace through an architectural link between them and those lost.

Here, in a quiet moment
between the stoic persistence of these arcing stone walls,
we might be tempted
to ask profound questions
at our own pace
and
within the space of our own hearts.

Falling Lotus Blossoms

Icons serve a special purpose across multiple scales of society and as such they should not be taken lightly. They require a unique design approach that seeks a match of symbolic representation to the culture and context they are intended to speak to. Icons are, by definition, intended to stand out, to inspire, to tell a story about the underlying entity or meaning which lend them validity. This invites the designer to strive for a thoughtful balance between constraint and exuberance. Icons must be sensitive to context, to consider how powerful the structure should be relative to its neighbors. In the case of Falling Lotus Blossoms, the site was, at the time it was designed, at the distant edge of a large city, a raw landscape extending out on three sides. Its iconic rationale was to celebrate India's first Economic Free Zone; an attempt to replicate China's success at creating economic abundance free of India's infamous bureaucratic morass.

Inspired by the white lotus, India's national flower, the design began as different iterations of the shape of the lotus flower petal. Ultimately, four "petals" were arranged like a four-leaf clover in plan with an open space at its center. In part a response to the extreme heat and humidity and the goal of populating the outdoor spaces for more than just a few months of the year, the buildings themselves contain semi-conditioned, shaded atrium spaces that serve as meeting or gathering spaces for the buildings' occupants. At dusk, each courtyard morphs into a giant kaleidoscope by the delineation of building elements with neon lighting.

Raised on the ground plane, the complex picks up a teleological dimension in that it becomes a quasi-temple devoted to the future of technology and its own iconography. As the eye follows the sweeping shape of the roof line, a vivid image of the fluid plane emerges. The building opens and embraces the users of a new society. This iconic project exemplifies technology as a transformative force for the language of architecture in a fast-growing country like India.

Located in the seventh largest metropolis in India, Falling Lotus Blossoms: EON IT Park is an elegantly arranged quartet of buildings that occupy a site located in the EON Free Zone, a Special Economic Zone established by the government to encourage development. This 21st-century workplace, which sets a grand scale in counterpoint to the rugged Indian countryside, overlooks a river and the fields beyond on a flat site that was previously almost entirely untouched.

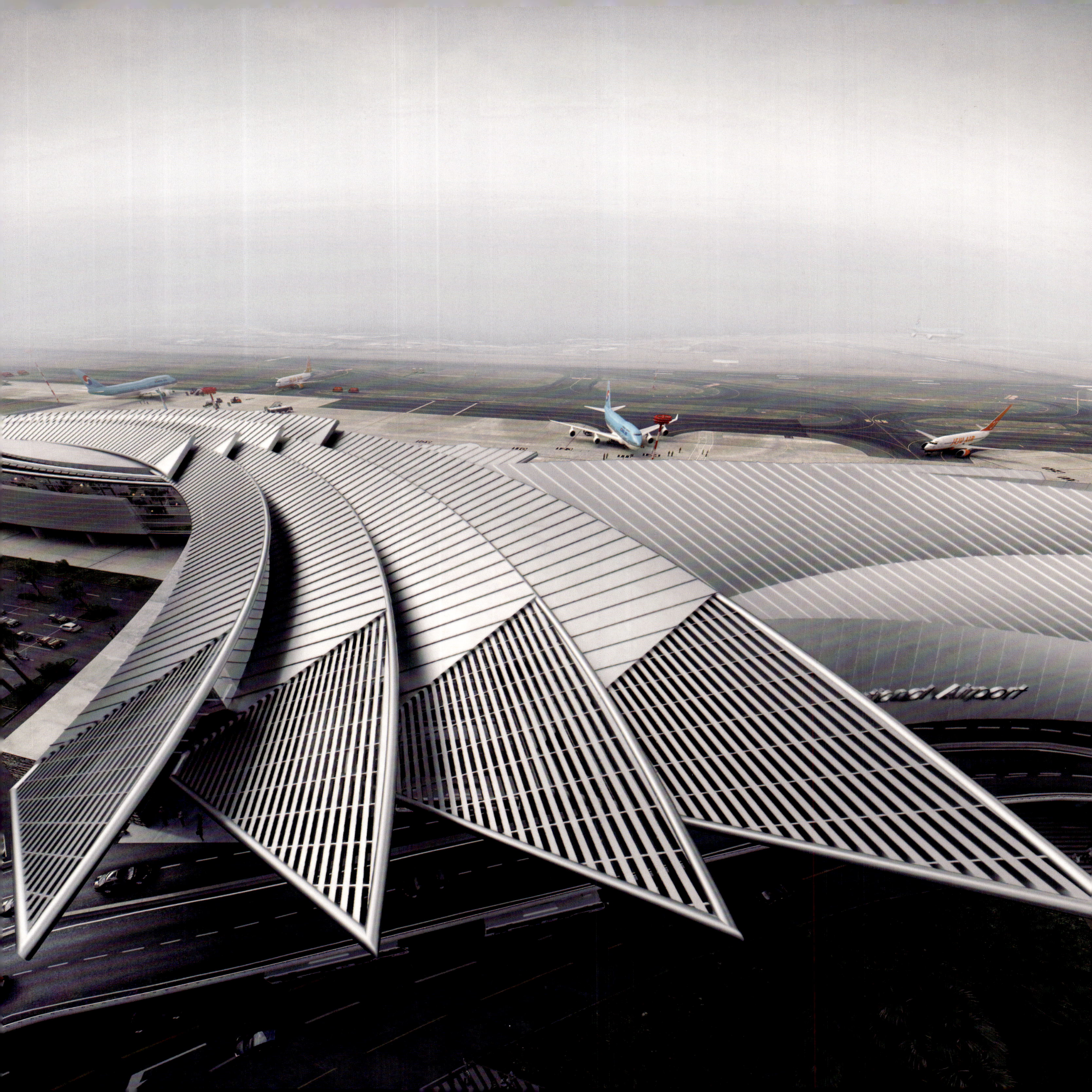

Portal of the Winds

Legend has it that winds formed the rocky and harsh landscape of Jeju Island before the first inhabitants ventured upon its shores. Centuries later, the island is known for its natural wonders and as a popular travel destination, so much so that it is the primary wedding and honeymoon spot in South Korea. The expansion and renovation of Jeju International Airport attempts to formalize the legacy of these strong winds responsible for the island's landscape.

The mystery of this project was how to fuse into a coherent design vision the geography of a region with aspiration for technological advancement. The contextual pressures of the site and nature were used as an inspirational source.

Broadly sweeping stainless steel roofs create a dynamic flow that expresses both the strength and beauty of the winds. As the defining design metaphor for the scheme, the winds determine the curvilinear geometry of the design. Throughout, the notion of wind is revealed in the massing of the addition, the shape of the canopies, and the circulation of the interiors.

Abstracted wind currents sculpt the interior and the exterior in the tripartite layout. This is realized in the design of the terminal ramp, particularly in the wings at the edges of the ramps that stretch the building horizontally to express the flow of users. Elsewhere, slanted cylindrical volumes and canted walls, reminiscent of local rocks and stones, suggest the coastline and encourage passengers to pause before they board the airplanes situated along the rounded plan.

Designed in collaboration with Jung-IL Architects

Few forces are as expressive
as the power of the wind to shape form,
yet
it is an ethereal flow
that eludes our human sight

JEJU
AIRPORT

There are many forms this might take; as in the act of providing housing for refugees, or in our case, as a proactive symbol of an imagined future, based on the tragedies of the past.

Embodied in this paid design competition entry is a sense of tension and repose, between the political wills of South and North Korea. The two arcing forms representing these two nations come together, at first with determined force and drama, but afterwards with the waters calming—blending back into one nation, one culture.

This also reflects the music and politics of composer Isang Yun, which the original concert hall was programmed to express. Midway through the design competition, the name and focus changed, from the Isang Yun Memorial Concert Hall to the Tongyeong International Concert Hall. This was a result of a change in the governing party of South Korea, which shifted from supportive of reunification to antagonistic. As a result, this design was not the one ultimately submitted by our team, led by a Korean conglomerate.

On an oceanside bluff that is exposed on all sides and has a view overlooking the

and vibrancy of Isang Yun's music. The name Crashing Waves establishes not only a strong tie to the site but evokes the composer's artistic intentions: to make out of clashing an ordering principle unbridled in its potential.

The upper level recalls the metaphorical frozen undulation of water waves, while the podium starts as a landform that mimics the ocean. The calm "water" at the base builds into a spatial crescendo culminating in the vertical glass elements that define the lobby. These elongated pieces become sculptural, slightly arching to become emblematic of "foam." The visual result is one of abstracted waves crashing together. This is unique and rare in nature but represents a powerful aspiration for many Koreans.

Fluidity endows the design with breathtaking dynamism. A series of fluid ramps stretch from the entry doors down to the parking lot. The reference to crashing waves informs the massing, section, and site plan.

Symbolically, it is the conflagration of the ocean, the music, and the two Koreas coming together that establishes the conceptual footprint that the plan is built upon, in tribute

Crashing Waves

Can architecture be a political act?

On some distant
seashore
Isang Yun sits
dreaming

of the day
two powerful
discordant
12 tone waves
will crash

their waters
mixing

aspiring to
an optimistic future

embracing
a tragic past

Lyrical Seashore

All great cities, in their golden eras, produce more culture and innovation than they consume. In order to create a world-class city, the creative vibrancy of the human spirit is front and center in the program for Kaohsiung Maritime Culture and Pop Music Center Design Competition.

The role of the designer is to breathe life into symbol and form that will capture the essence of a place and its aspirations towards a collective future. To achieve this, Lyrical Seashore embraces the city's harbor in one sweeping move. On this prominent tray of liminal land, Lyrical Seashore intensifies the urban pulse of the populace with a string of activity.
The sensuous yet logical form of sea creatures, ships, and the fluidity of music are the three themes drawn from the program and the site, setting the tone for a seductive spatiality and repertoire of shapes.

Once the site of a small lagoon in the 1640s, the port grew into a major export harbor of agricultural products during Japanese rule in the first half of the 20th century and then into one of the world's top container ports. Lyrical Seashore was designed as a catalyst to once again transform the port, celebrating its historical importance and encouraging its further growth into a major tourism, trade, and transit port.

Two branches of facilities run alongside an indoor concert hall and outdoor performance area. Facing the city, the project appears like a two-story curtain of architectural objects, with portals functioning as public plazas protecting views of the water. Containing a dense network of retail and restaurant elements, as well as large cultural institutions, the most significant is a string of individual performance spaces between the auditoria, which houses restaurants, shops, and a recording studio at the tail end along the denser side of the city. These elements blend into a necklace of buildings that are activated from day to night.

The Marine Culture Exhibit Center, a music innovation center and a prominent leaning "sail-like" observation tower that, at 200-meters tall, will become a new landmark on the city's skyline.

Throughout the project, large curving sun canopies are covered with photovoltaics to produce on-site energy. The existing curvilinear railway line is used as a bicycle path, and the shape of the site itself triggers the fluid geometry of the final form.

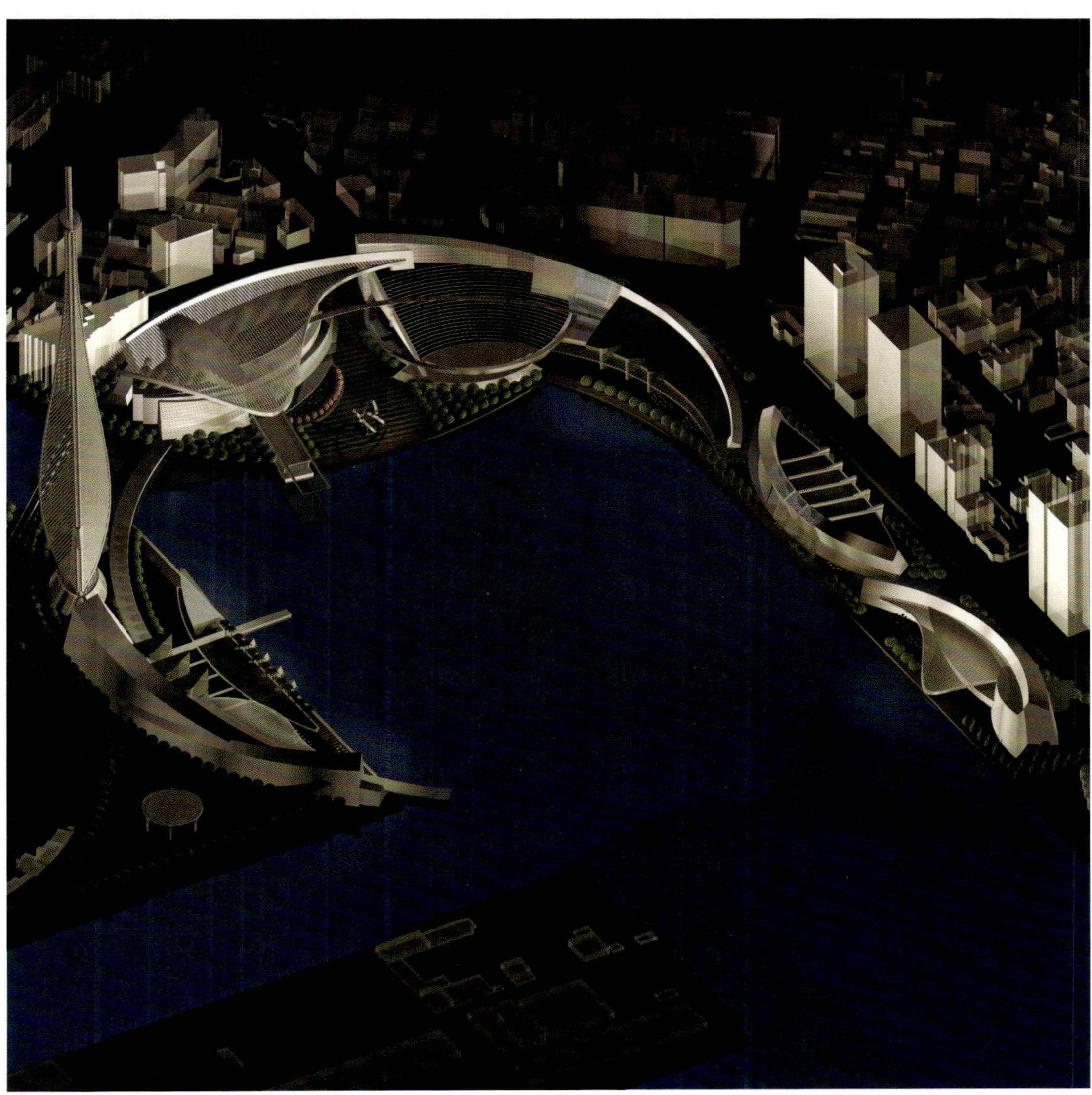

Sanguine Lily

Some architectural commissions and competitions provide an opportunity for sacred dialogue, to memorialize a profound moment in the journey of humankind.

The Easter Rising in 1916 marked the inevitable rise of Ireland's political independence. The insurrection lasted only five days but was a momentous call for freedom. Following the uprising, 232 casualties were buried by the British in a mass grave in the Glasnevin Cemetery. The 1916 Centenary Chapel at Glasnevin Cemetery is designed as a beacon of hope, a lighthouse in the darkness of unmanageable events.

The design builds on the rich symbolism of the Easter lily, which represents peace, to shape a place of cleansing or renewal of vows. In addition to paying homage to the 232 lives lost, the chapel design aims to bring together and unify the greater Dublin community, acting as a portal for lost loved ones, while also being a symbol of indissoluble unity amongst the living.

Surrounded on three sides by a reflecting pool, a metaphoric baptismal font, the chapel appears from afar to be a petal floating on a puddle of water. The bridges from the grassy fields to the chapel link the profane to the sacred.

Symbolism is found in every aspect of the design. Inside the chapel, a massive stone alter invokes the heaviness of the past, with the graveyard behind, while the lightness and transparency of the glass walls suggest the temptation towards an optimistic future. Indeed, a major focal point of the Centenary Chapel is the use of light in the structure. Natural light streams in from the north and south through glass curtain walls that enclose the chapel, allowing for maximum luminosity during the day.

At night, 232 glass sphere lights suspended from the ceiling each represent a soul ascending to heaven and form a luminous crown visible in the nocturnal sky, giving visual form to their ultimate sacrifice thus making the chapel a perpetual beacon of unity and reflection for city dwellers. To remember and to give hope.

The east-west orientation of the chapel axis is generative of a longitudinal space sitting on an elliptical water basin, this being a metaphorical baptismal font sponsoring the renewal of the vows of Irish people to the country's independence. In this arrangement, the mass grave becomes the focal point on the north side, visually integrated into the chapel's experience.

The Centenary Chapel aims at joining the past, present, and future in a way that makes a perfect moment shaped into an elegant and refined structure that will stand resolutely for all to experience.

A corona of 232 glass spheres represents the indissoluble passion to fight oppression in all its pervasive forms

Glass Butterfly

Bus shelters are atypical building types. In the mind of the collective, their utilitarian purpose relegates them to the realm of outdoor accessories, or, to paraphrase Le Corbusier's famous dictum, they are "machines for waiting." They sit somewhere in major thoroughfares, uncommitted to the specificity of their location. The standard approach is that one look fits all sites, but this is a risky proposition for an increasingly ubiquitous object crowding the public realm.

For a design competition organized by a glazing manufacturing company, the programmatic purpose was to create an all-glass design for a bus shelter in a rural area of Denmark. Rather than following the standard approach driven by mere function, the Glass Butterfly is inspired by a formal negotiation between the delicacy of glass and its structural integrity.

The design wanted to be self-referential and authoritative in the landscape. Trees, weaving grass, and big canopies were key inspirational organic forms. The gentle nature of the Danish environment became the source for the proposed biomorphic volume. Like a graceful butterfly, this structure radiates its immaterial presence to its surroundings day and night. This scalable transparent container, almost a frozen membrane, is a place of protection, sheltering users from rain, wind, and sun.

Despite its seemingly imminent flight from the ground, this artifact is securely anchored to the soil through unobtrusive steel connections. Maximum structural integrity is provided by the graceful, U-shaped glass bays. The bays are scalable to afford a variety of seating arrangements for those who are alone, couples, or groups of friends, with deep protection from wind and rain.

The elliptical photovoltaic panels laid on the roof and directly above the bays have the dual function of harnessing solar energy to power the structure and serving as sunshading devices to shield those sitting below.

The structure morphs from a simple portal between here and there, to an oasis. As an easily identifiable billboard and beacon, the glass medium provides a point of belonging. It transitions from a transparent cocoon serving the occupants' need to see out and catch the approaching vehicle during the day, to a guidepost at night. It is for this reason that linear LED lighting follows the edges of the canopy, illuminating its architecture even in complete Nordic darkness.

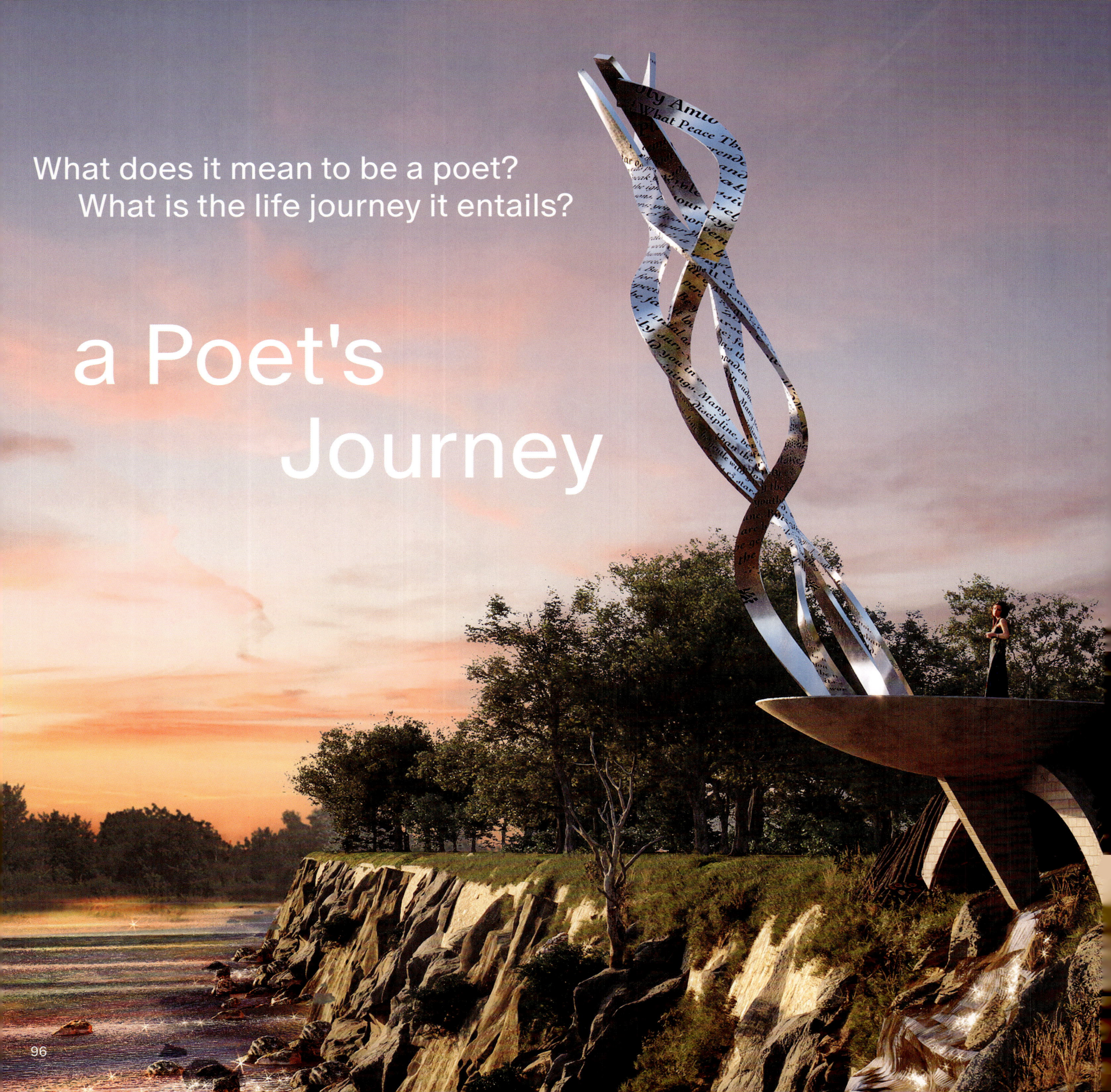

What does it mean to be a poet?
What is the life journey it entails?

a Poet's Journey

For this romanticized monument to poetry, reposed on an eastern bluff overlooking the Mississippi river, our design is fundamentally experiential, a sequence of experiences, each expressed by a series of symbols. The design reflects on what it means to be a poet and on the lifelong journey it entails. It starts with a sylvan sense of innocence, of life's potential, ending with an inverted homage to Arnold Böcklin's famous painting *Isle of the Dead*.

This journey begins by wandering through an Arcadian forest representing one's early life experience. As one's journey progresses, the forest becomes denser, more complicated, harder to navigate, reflecting the wild, raw, and sometimes absurd nature of the world. At some point in this journey, a faint path might appear, partially hidden, more of a temptation than a direction, or the result of an epiphany.

Here the young poet emerges and starts to find their voice. They encounter a partially ruined colonnade, representing human and cultural history. Next is an ascending incline, made of charred wood, the fire that burns in our hearts. To the right are a set of three pedestals, each containing an ever-changing array of the building blocks of the art of poetry. To the left, there is a large rock with a hidden sitting area, where one can contemplate the absurdities and joys of the world. After some time, when the poet is ready, they rise and walk out onto a reflecting pool, where their words flow forth in ribbons of stainless steel.

Should the poet, still curious about the mysteries of life, wander out towards the river, they might encounter a space of true solitude, built into the base of the monument—a Poet's Cave, a place that will protect your heart, at its most tender moments. This is the creative phase of a journey, when words flow like sweet water from our lips.

The final aspect of this journey is to descend a series of steps, hard cut into the rocky cliff-side. At the bottom of the steps is a stone pier. Silence is your witness as you wait for what might happen next. In due time, a soft light appears in the river mists. As it comes closer, one can see a lantern on the bow of a small boat, a silent figure shrouded in white comes to take you across a strangely calm river.

trickery.
Be yoursel
about love;
perennial
gracefully

House of Borrowed Light

Intimate and personal, the House of Borrowed Light centers around the interplay between adjacencies and relationships, fluidity and translucency.

True to its name, the design for this penthouse brings light back to the north-facing residence since the front door enters into the darkest part of the apartment. This programmatic priority led to borrowing light from everywhere else in order to deliver it to the depths of the internal connective tissue. Glass surfaces partition space in a careful balance between delivering privacy and allowing in natural light. The design is a study of the sensuous potentials of translucent glass, playing that delicacy off solid forms in wood, stone, and painted wall.

The penthouse provides an opportunity for placemaking on two levels:

The first is the metaphoric sense of its location in the context of San Francisco. Environmental themes unique to the microclimate of San Francisco, such as the infamous swirling fog of the Bay Area, drove shapes, material surfaces with etched glass, and the curving forms into spatial dialogue with each other.

The second is the penthouse in the context of the client's life. There is a custom mural that references his family's history when they escaped mainland China.

Sea Song

In the immeasurable natural beauty of Big Sur on the California coast, Sea Song is unobtrusive by design; it is both private from the main road and utterly transparent to what lies ahead. Likened to a trio of gliding manta rays, its environmental footprint is virtually nil and causes minimum disturbance to the site.

The sculpturally minimalistic geometry of the three pavilions is fluid, unbroken, and in motion. Their arrangement provides a continuum with no set boundaries between the inside and the outside. Internally, it is an immaterial enclosure with no corridors, only livable space. The three structures are alike in mass and architectural elements but scaled differently to adhere to the specific program requirements. Concrete core anchors forms to the earth where the programmatic parts reside. Everything else floats in inebriating lightness. In each, the enclosed concrete split core holds service functions, giving maximum open areas to the mostly column-free surrounding vistas.

Every chance to open the sightlines to the ocean was taken in these natural lyrical forms. In entering each pavilion at their midpoint, a gap between the heavy concrete cores gives glimpses of the vastness to expect beyond that threshold, anticipation and reward upon coming inside. The interior surfaces exhibit refined and warm natural materials and carefully positioned art pieces, yet are purposefully left plain to become background to its majestic outside. Wood roofs float ethereally above the concrete cores with a delicate lightness of touch.

The house is an architectural creature breathing with its natural surroundings. This trio of spaces is designed to be self-sustaining, net zero energy, and aims at LEED Platinum certification. The full array of sustainable techniques is employed, consolidating the architecture as a natural extension of this site. Photovoltaics ease off-the-grid living. Self-cleaning glass, rainwater retention cistern, and xeriscape secure the sensible use of water sources. The landscaping is intentionally kept nonformal to reinforce the intent that Sea Song has always belonged to this site.

In the immeasurable natural beauty of Big Sur
this harmonic
of solid and light
grounds a sense of belonging
of being an integral part of this earth

Luminous Moon Gate

The luminous grace of knowledge is the surest pathway toward a charting of the future. This is as true now as it was a millennium ago. Knowledge, when combined with culture, becomes a powerful platform for improving the human condition. These two, in dynamic balance, are in many ways the essence of all change.

In traditional Chinese iconography, a moon gate symbolizes a gateway "to the Garden of Paradise." In today's Information Age, this paradise may aspire to be a future where knowledge and culture shape humankind in profound ways. For the 2013 Taichung City Cultural Center International Competition, we designed the "Luminous Moon Gate," in which the combination of a library and a museum is uniquely suited to provide the basis for this future.

The design intent behind the proposed project hints at multiple interpretative roles for Taichung: a portal into heightened consciousness, a lantern of knowledge, a catalyst for metropolitan living, a cultural lung for the body of the city, a gate toward a responsible future, a center regenerative of community life, a landmark for orientation.

The project replaces various military installations and the former Shuinan airport, as most of these functions have been discontinued. Located on the northern end of the new Taichung Gateway Park, the library and the museum act as both a singular cultural landmark and entrance to the greater urban park. Each building axis points to pivotal parts of the park and the city.

The library, the vertical oval, and the museum, the horizontal oval, work in tandem to express the concept of gateway, yet are distinct volumes with shared design language. One is counterpoint to the other and laid out programmatically, the former vertically and the latter horizontally. The buildings feature largely glass surfaces that draw passersby throughout the day and serve as a beacon of activity at night, following the idea that transparency of knowledge leads to collective achievements.

The Grand Stair is an allegory (with a nod to Ledoux) of the power of knowledge, accessible to all citizens of a free society. Majestic in scale, it marks the entry point to the Great Forum of the library, drawing the public to ascend and reach the long view on all human matters. This transparent landmark extends the compositional axis of the Taichung Gateway Park. The rich imagery of the architecture of the Enlightenment shapes the dominant forms of this scheme. This marker is a two-way signal: cascading knowledge and culture from the complex to the public realm, and channeling the urban dwellers from the street to its institutional void.

The vertical culmination of the library is the Great Reading Room, the architectural center where knowledge gets internalized. In the vastness of its vault, patrons and visitors gather to learn, to experience, to open to the city below. Education, personal growth, citizenship, and the fostering of the arts will regain center stage in the life of Taichung. The Great Reading Room affords expansive views of the city and Taichung Gateway Park. From the street level it is a destination, the place to be—from up there, it is the vantage point to discover.

Cloudscape

A skyline is what defines a city on the horizon. Most often it is composed of an assemblage of high-rise buildings that are recognizable in the urban fabric as a point of pride. Tall and slender, these structures offer the opportunity to soar, literally "in the clouds," and when they are designed at their best, they can create an emotional presence. They give an urban skyline its character, and, in a sense, they form the cultural symbol of a city—of what it aspires to be and where it sees the future.

Cloudscape takes the abstracted form of cumulus clouds as its symbolic reference. This has two origins. The first is a reference to the natural world, to the fog and mists that permeate the city of San Francisco. The second inspiration comes from the cloud computing technology that is fueling unprecedented global change and in San Francisco has created an impact that rivals the Gold Rush of 1849.

Its design follows a classic base, middle, and top structure. The base is a study in humane scale. The long western street frontage is bisected by a 40-foot-wide passage through the building and is paired with an iconic lobby that takes the form of a 60-foot sphere emerging from the ground and making its way towards the sky. The space between this project and its neighbor is celebrated with a broad paseo that follows a grand arc, connecting a new south midblock alley to an eastern midblock alley. This network of spaces is activated by incorporating indoor and outdoor retail, pedestrian-oriented service, and dining spaces into the public realm.

The middle section of the tower is an elegant shaft with a distinctly vertical articulation, which accentuates a feeling of ascension, of clouds forming and rising to the sky. The shaft is interrupted by two shapes. The first is a protruding sphere, and a bit further up is the reverse, a 60-foot diameter void with a razor-thin circular platform extending out, creating a viewing deck and midlevel aspirational space.

On an urban scale, the emotional intent for the building's crown is expressed by a mysterious and tumultuous form—part technological wonder, part natural allusion. The top eight stories are ethereal, like a vapor. A harmonic arrangement of 30 glass spheres, of varying diameters, form the basis for this metaphor. Within this composition of soaring bubbles are vast sky gardens, and public and private spaces, including cafes, exhibition rooms, and meeting and work areas.

Here, the horizon is raised to match the aspiration to leave a meaningful imprint in a world we want to change for the better. It is in Cloudscape that we find a spot from where to dream bigger dreams, acquire perspective, and organize our thoughts, protected from the elements while in the midst of nature—ready to make a creative mark in the sky.

ONE

Innovation Curve

The dynamic architecture of the Innovation Curve at Stanford Research Park celebrates the creative process of technology, which is fundamental to the international success of Silicon Valley. The two-story peaks and valleys of sweeping blue metal curves serve as architectural metaphors for the highs and lows of exploratory research and development; creative sparks and the pragmatic analysis of ideas descend to transition into long, horizontal bands symbolizing the implementation phase of invention.

The new campus comprises four buildings on the edge of Stanford Research Park in Palo Alto. The LEED Platinum-certified project contributes to the site's emergence as an uplifting campus for tenants involved with computer gaming, translation software, bio tech, and digital inventions. Representing the evolution of innovation on the face of the buildings, the lyrical design serves as a potent visual reminder of the dedicated, expansive, and intense work taking place inside.

The Innovation Curve buildings are arranged around a central landscaped courtyard with diagonal pedestrian paths leading from adjacent streets through the site. Each of the four color-coded buildings comprises two offset wings flanking a central, glass-faced lobby to break up the building mass. In the lobby, both the concrete courtyard paving and metal curves of the building exteriors extend through the two-story space to create a sculptural portal connected to the outdoors.

On the building exterior, projecting roofs and deep overhangs—fabricated of painted recycled aluminum—are configured to capture the forward-leaning spirit of technology. Thus, the process of creativity is made visible in three dimensions. The overhangs curve downward to low points near the ground to represent the challenging process of risk assessment, market financing, and decision-making. From there, they rise to the ends of each building to express an uplifting conclusion to the innovation diagram. These projecting planes supply outdoor balconies offering vistas of the campus and the bits-and-bytes world outside the technology park.

In addition to their symbolic significance, the deep overhangs show that green design can be light, sophisticated, and lyrical by working in combination with vertical glass fins to shade the building exteriors, control solar heat gain, and allow for greater transparency and connection to campus life.

The old Library

sat low in the land
with the warmth of an old lodge, out west
wood and brick
with a fireplace
that was never lit
but carried the romantic remnants
of past times when it was used extensively
so easy
to envision an evening of storytelling around a fire
with the indulgence of hot cocoa

the park seeped in from corner windows
making the landscape appear to effortlessly flow inside
while
a full-height glass wall led you out
to an expansive brick terrace
where you could read a book
in the sun
surrounded
by flowers
and birds

and the distant sounds of cable cars

promised was the future
a better building
more suited to a modern library
where we could enjoy the comforts
of an efficient mechanical system

It's an all-white space now

with towering 20-foot ceilings
that lofty drama
exciting at first...now unsustaining

the reading room
lost heart of my prior experience
lacks focus and delight
save that every point
can be monitored from a security desk

there are rows of tables
efficiently laid out
like a factory for working on essays
about effectiveness without passion

I miss
the reading room
the quiet corners
was a refuge from my parents and siblings
the little nooks of intimacy
it felt like a second home
the old wood beams and brick
more luxurious than my own
that was harder to maintain
this quiet place
where your mind could rest
but made me feel loved
then run wild
Somehow the architects missed the warmth
It's all gone now
forgot to add a sense of belonging
a sense
after a long-pitched battle
between the future
of a place you just could relax in for hours
and dream about the worlds these books hinted at
people who thought the old building was tired
and dated
Now it feels like a fast-food restaurant
didn't fit into the neighborhood because it had
the space waiting
to push you back onto the street again
'50s hip roof
do your business and let the next customer in
in a sea of Victoriana
except no one seems to come here much anymore

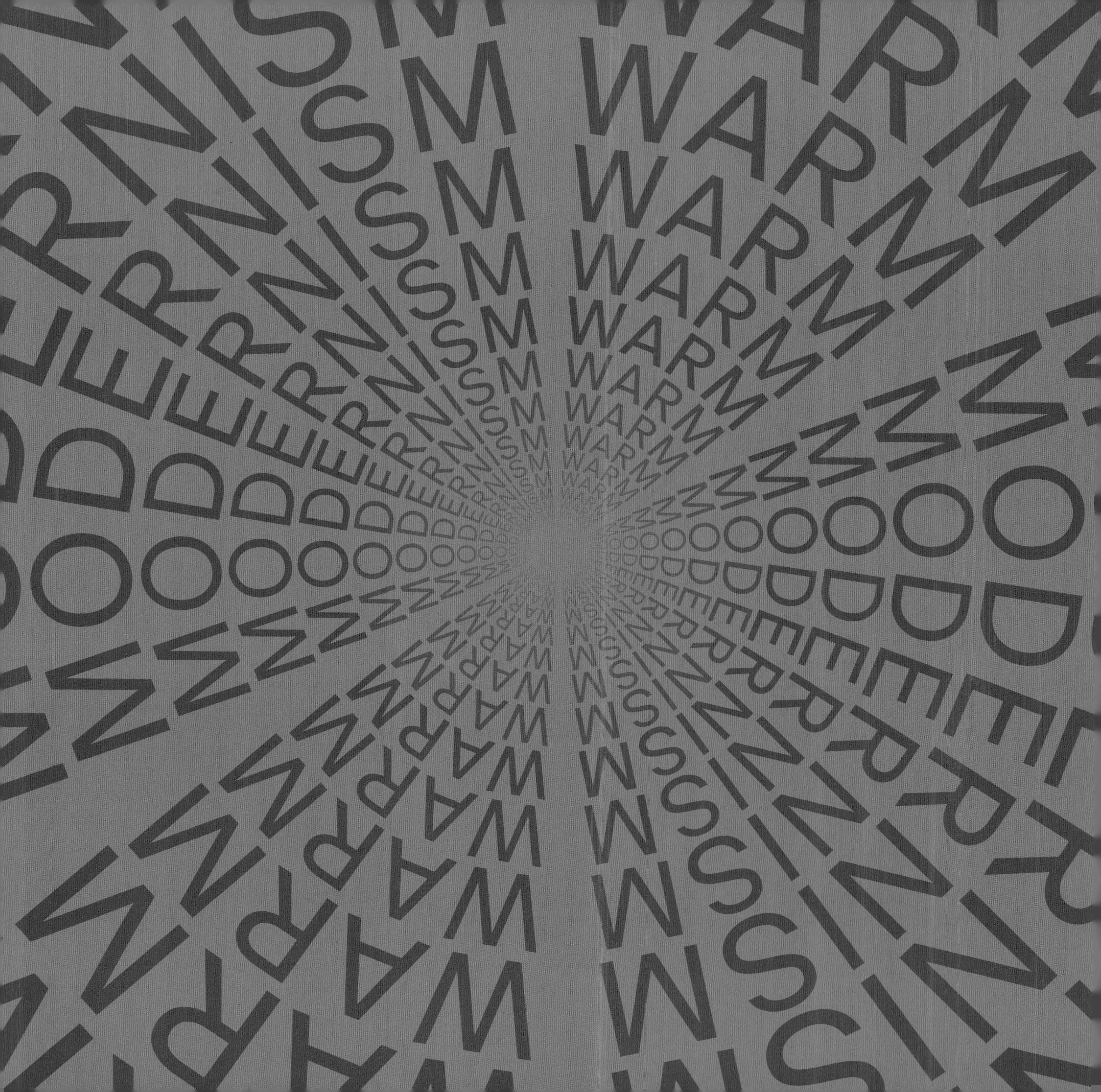
WARM MODERNISM

Modernism as a style has a fascinating and tumultuous history. There was an imaginative and intuitive quality to the design ethos of early modernism that imbued a rich and deeply human character. Initially this was an act of rebellion: stylistically, culturally, socially, economically, politically.

Modernism represented a vision of the future and potential of humanity to soar to great heights, freed from the shackles of past conventions and past atrocities. We believed in that future. We believed that humankind could conquer disease and poverty and have dominion over nature. Eventually, the law of unintended consequences caught up to us, leading to an unhealthy state of extreme imbalance; an arrogance that thinking was the highest order of human achievement.

We drifted toward conceptual clarity, intellectual rigidity, a machine architecture; and away from joy and warmth, away from expressing the human heart. Architects started to remove beauty and grace from their palate in an effort to be taken seriously. Caught in a conflict between art and business, the profession of architecture seemed to fall victim to a pragmatic materialism disguised as philosophical and theoretical integrity. A blandness emerged in the form of Non-Poetic Minimalism. Design is most memorable and relevant when there is a human uniqueness to its expression We need to reach back to the early moments of Modernism, back to when we believed in the future, but rather than a future solely based on rationalism and technology, we need to add back poetry and the warmth of the human spirit.

Modernism, as a style, is quite capable of producing lovable and inspiring buildings. It takes a very simple effort; that of an intention of empathy. Warm Modernism is an opportunity to open up the stylistic range of normative minimalism, and to regain the relevancy of design to the public. It explores the joy of graphic composition in elevation, trades beauty for conceptual consistency. It includes detailing that might be considered decorative, balancing richness of experience with cleverness, and creating a hierarchy of interest in form and texture.

Warm Modernism imparts a balanced approach, focusing on a calmness, but with a heart, and a richness of interest, rather than the emptiness of Non-Poetic Minimalism. In Warm Modernism, the whole makes you feel welcomed and loved, comfortable and cared for.

Where the Birds Sing

Reversing the typical proportional relationship between buildings and landscape, a set of carefully crafted pavilions gently dots an expansive pastoral scene, while retaining the confidence of its architectural language the human-made is purposefully enmeshed in the natural world. Large swaths of the campus were left natural, so that the embrace of nature is all encompassing and calibrated to offer an array of experiences to those who visit. From secret gardens hidden in the crevices of the architecture to the robust scale of the campus green, these episodic adventures expand and contract organically in size to enable personal ways of dwelling in space, which are all evocative while offering a variety of landscape experiences.

By separating the road from the workplace, we created a car-free campus. More than just about environmental stewardship, it creates an opportunity for the entire campus to encounter each other the same way.

We separated the large hilltop site into neighborhoods with lyrical names: Hilltop, Promontory, and Creekside. This provided the opportunity to give each section a unique and special quality, in balance with an intention to maintain some common design threads. The areas are tied together as a coherent whole by a magnificent axis, the Grand Allée, graced with moving water and laid out along the east-west direction. The Grand Allée traverses the site from the highest point of the campus to the lowest point in a series of straight lines, linking together over half of the campus's buildings.

In searching for the spirit of Palo Alto's rich mid-century modern design history and cultural zeitgeist, we designed the structures with a horizontal emphasis and long elegant roofs and deep overhangs. To add warmth, we used stone accents in critical places. We reduced the size to a semi-residential scale; each building became a village of buildings. With a weightless origami quality, the roof forms look as if they were a creature in flight or the edge of an airplane wing. The ends of the buildings also open themselves in a classic Californian way, with full-height glass walls that create a sense of welcome and connection to the beauty of the landscape.

Layered Grace

For decades a stronghold of background historicism, Silicon Valley has steadily morphed into a land of modernism, albeit with two significant differences. It is modeled on a human scale and is tailored to people's needs rather than to impersonal users. This entity has been an urban contradiction with no credible explanation of its built predicament since the decline of the military industrial complex in the 1960s. Silicon Valley is the symbolic capital of an industry grounded in imagining the future, but it has appeared to be incapable of living it in its own physical premises. Corporate headquarters are now choosing a more consistent message for their overarching philosophy. They are the future of the communication infrastructure and want to express it in the architecture they inhabit. Netflix's second headquarters is proof of such profound change of attitude toward the built environment. Their first headquarters was a Tuscan-esque acquiescence to perceived local cultural requirements. The second campus tested that perception with a voter referendum, and a sense of warm modernism prevailed.

Headquarters' four buildings are designed to be delicate and genteel. A slender bridge located midair connects them, thus preserving their identities as individual structures. The tripartite facade has the imaginative interplay of aluminum fins, deep overhangs, and silver metal panels. The punched openings carved against the terracotta-colored precast panels intertwine with the modern curtain wall system.

The design for Netflix's new headquarters is unabashedly eclectic and wide-ranging in its use of materials and stylistic changes to create warmth and richness of experience—from metal, to wood, to bold colors. Inside, the design intentionally blurs the separation between work, social, and eating areas. Relaxed and collaborative work-spaces, emulating residences, are created using dividers, warm colors, and textures. The first-floor cafeteria, the main social space, pours out into a secure courtyard. An intimate fireplace, a waterfall wall creating a privacy nook, lush ceilings, and wall treatments are all part of the rich features and textures of the private, collaborative, and social spaces.

The vibrant and dynamic palette was enhanced by skillful collaboration in designing custom light fixtures, which serve to landmark key functions in the building. These lighting motifs create artistic statements in their own right. The result is a very user-friendly, welcoming environment with a generous visual interest and high-functioning yet efficient space layout.

The exterior landscaping of the courtyard and the walkway bridge that spans above it allow for a free flow from building to building. The garden defines the general experience of this project as a place. Mature redwood trees ranging from 40 feet to 100 feet in height planted along a linear garden add to the bucolic character of the complex. They confer spatial majesty through their sheer size, with the architecture of the campus being a benevolent complement to its natural message.

Overlaid Harmonies

Situated halfway between San Francisco and San Jose, Redwood City is a place in active pursuit of an updated urban identity. Neither a fully colonized outpost for tech companies nor a suburban dormitory for commuters to both cities, this is a town seeking a recognizable presence.

A carefully crafted blend of the modern and traditional informs the design of this urban infill project. Set on the edge of the historicist downtown, it speaks to the future while respecting the past. The project brings warmth, texture, and richness of detail and articulation to the building massing. Precast panels, which look like terracotta, a layering of reveals, mullions, and metal trim make the articulated elegance of a building skin as refined as it is cultivated in its architectural references. Every element fits together with precision and gracefulness.

In styling the otherwise squarish facades, great attention is paid to building up a crescendo toward the upper level. There, the glass is recessed 6 feet back to create a generous linear terrace linked to a grand balcony in the back of the structure. That cushion of glass and the deep shadow from the stepped back treatment is what makes the roof float.

550
550

The building's verticality is most pronounced at the intersection of Fuller and Winslow Streets, where the resulting acute angle triggers an upward thrust raising the roof hovering on the glassed corner. This powerful gesture is the dynamic termination of the sculptural roof element, which starts at the building's two disparate entries, dramatically angling up the elevation to the roofline, continuous and distinctive against the skyline. Evocative of expressionist architecture, the formal tension of this specific moment in the design signals the apex in a scheme. In contributing to the urban character of the neighborhood, this is conceived as a city building, courteous to the adjacent structures, but with an attitude about itself.

Mondrian's Window

In Roman mythology, Janus is a god with two faces, one looking toward the future and the other toward the past. Similarly, this rear addition to a one-bedroom house represents a creative front where artwork is carried out, whereas the existing part—allocated to routine functions—faces the street.

The design symbolizes the architecture of linearity and sequence, where all of the rooms across the three stories have a sightline, progressively more expansive as one moves higher, overlooking a downward-sloping garden and panoramas of the Bay.

The rear elevation, now the primary facade of the house, is rich in explicit formal references. They range from the Dutch cabinet maker/architect Gerrit Rietveld for volumetric composition, to Dutch painter Piet Mondrian for the subdivision of the glazing and its coloring, and contemporary New York architect Richard Meier for the expression of frames containing the individual windows in and out of the primary building envelope.

Through a language of planes, a much larger scale is hinted at than what the current footprint really affords. In breaking down the smaller elements, blatant symmetry is avoided while simultaneously remaining elusive. As a result, there is some symmetry in the middle floor, wherein the sectional ins and outs activate the default flatness of the elevation. Selective use of dichroic glass suggests further scale as a pursuit of optical vibrancy. These bold primary colors are repeated in the two main worktables' bright-colored glass tabletops, as well other furniture selections. Rather than follow a prescriptive palette of primaries, the eastern wall surfaces are broken up into planes in an homage to the colors of the California morning. Muted yellow, green, and blue make their way through all three floors to create a sense of unity. These colors also reflect the chromatic range of the artist resident's work.

The addition provides an abundance of natural light in the creative spaces and the original areas gain more breathing room while continuing to cater to everyday functions. These areas were kept in the Edwardian/Arts and Crafts style in deference to two generations of artists who lived in the house prior to the current owners.

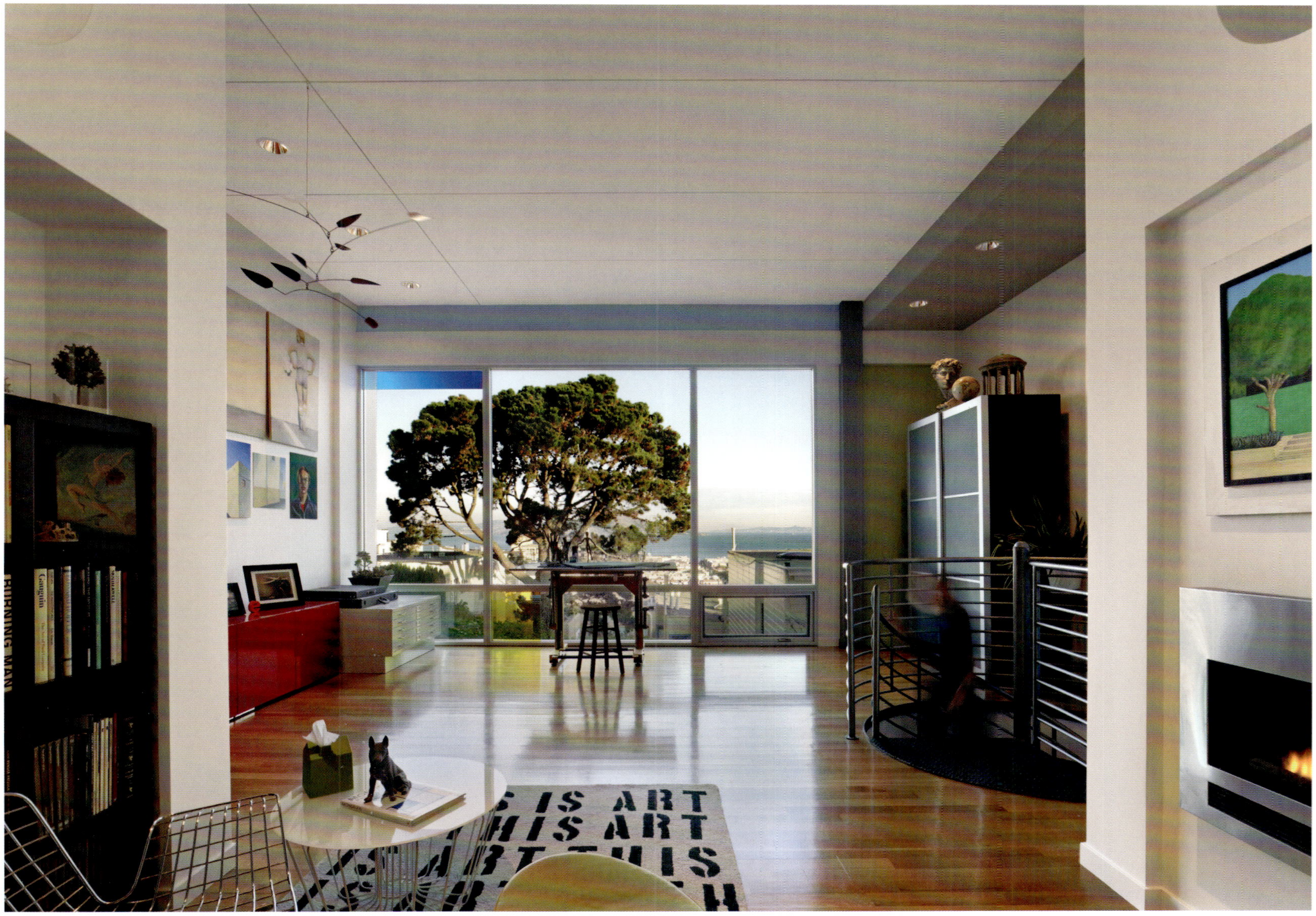
IS ART
HIS ART

THIS IS ART

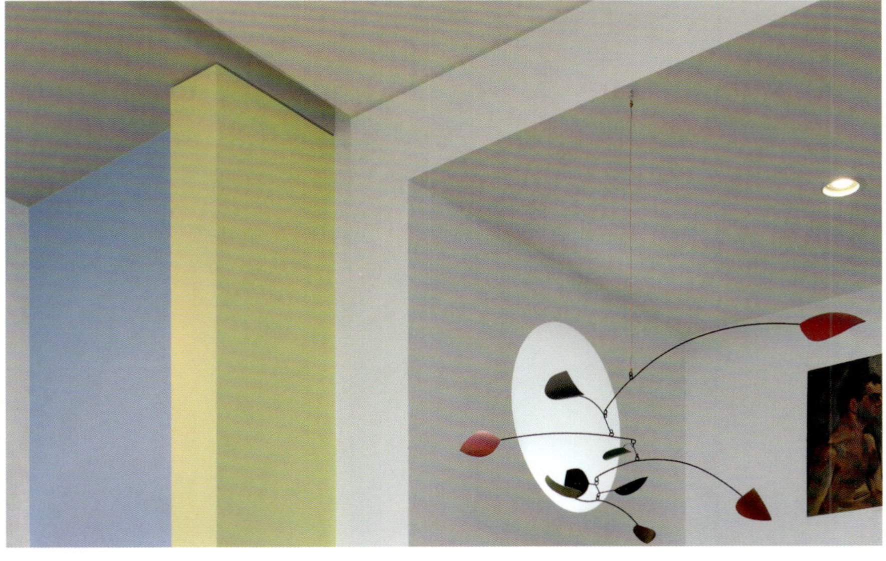

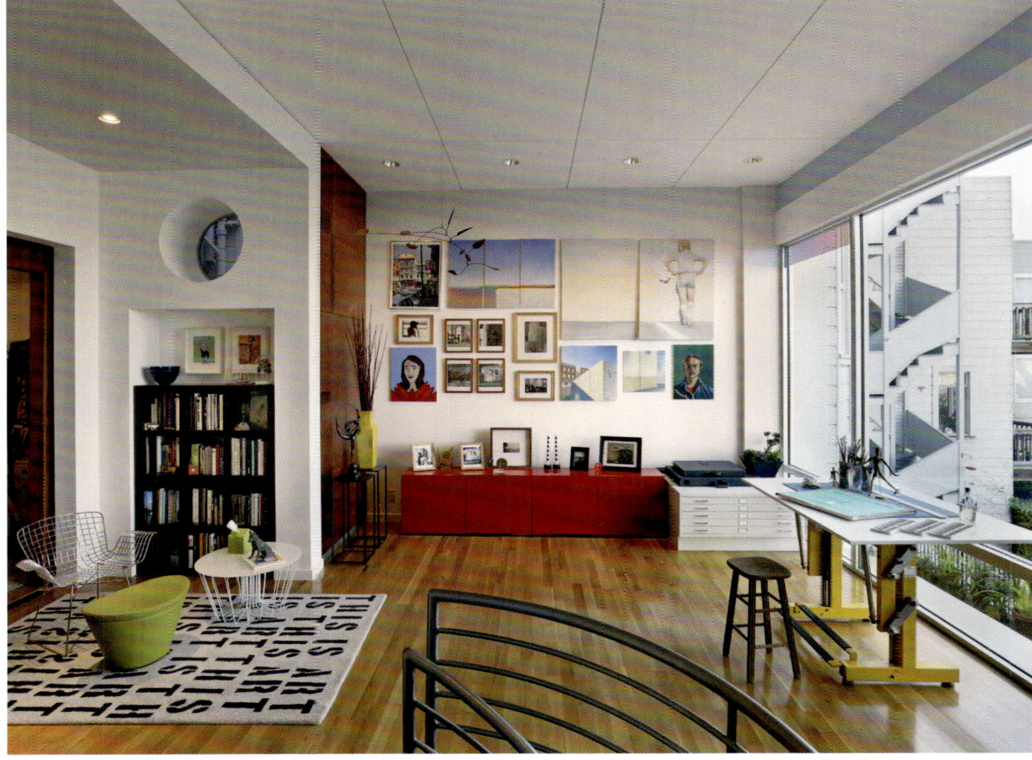

Friedlander

Urban Frames

Inhabiting Palo Alto is an experience straddling worldly urbanity and American sprawl. Together with the suburban feel detectable as you step further away from University Avenue, the town's main street, there is distinct character, human scale, lush nature, and pedestrian friendliness in its neighborhoods. This housing/office project aims to present an image that is both distinct and belonging to its place.

Distinctive volumes, conceived as an architectural ensemble, articulate their own skyline against the pronounced horizontality of Palo Alto. They occupy a quarter of a city block, offering to the local community a restrained Mediterranean modernity, disciplined and relaxed at the same time. Its cubist massing lets coexist individuality in multiplicity: each unit has a recognizable presence while being fully integrated into a total vision. Earthbound, yet light and powerfully extruded to a majestic height, these voided boxes are the markers of an architecture with no back of house: all elevations relate meaningfully to their adjacencies. This boxy geometry reinforces the corners of the lot, making of axiality a flexible rule for a lively architectural composition.

This is a new design language in the architecture of Palo Alto. Hardscape and landscape knit together the building footprints into a continuum in the manner of an old European city, an effective idea tested in centuries of urban design practices. There is a permeability that is designed into the separation of the live and work blocks, reflecting one of Palo Alto's great urban charms, that of a network of intimate alleyways and hidden gardens.

Outdoor spaces at midair are evocative of balconies. To invite pedestrians to inhabit any architecture is to coax them into an experience filled with interest, safety, and surprise. An environment in which to gather, share, retreat, entertain, nurture, reflect, work, and function. In a nutshell, a place.

I tend to ignore the press about new buildings after years of disappointment the words
and restraint when it misses the poetry that makes those rare buildings sing always
the entrance because there is a door handle on an otherwise undifferentiated glass
center Jaded I envisioned a Disneyesque pandering with too many lights and
nothing was real or authentic There are times in your life when you can be wrong
spot it seems it's all about balance of constraint and exuberance of rigor and
this building instead of picking one side of a binary of resolving a paradox by discarding
seemingly opposing elements in the spirit of that ancient adage: the whole is greater
to this design where the architects let loose let the quirky personality of multiple
of adventure without resorting to the excesses of Las Vegas or Dubai It had the charm
places to watch to eat to play to hide to assemble a crowd and dance Every
texture hoping the magic would never end (we used to know how to make magic)

I wish I lived closer

sounding so sweet only to find the reality underwhelming and uninspired simplicity
leaves me wondering why I wasted an afternoon Like a building where you can only find
wall There were rumors this building was FUN it was a large market hall, a new town
garish sentimentality of overselling vibrancy past the point of distraction where
about everything between the extremes of banality and overstimulation there is a sweet
playfulness of refinement and innovation of abstraction and abundance Here in
what didn't fix the expected outcome this architect fully embraced this duality balanced
than the sum of the parts its strength in the surprise and delight There is a sweetness
designers create a wonderful sense of humanity and grace It manifests a lively sense
of an ancient city with a crisp modernism that engaged your sense of joy There were
nook and cranny invites you to explore a never-ending creativity of form and
I want to go back there spend a lazy afternoon wandering or just being

BALANCE
BALANCE
DYNAMIC
BALANCE
BALANCE
BALANCE
BALANCE
DYNAMIC
BALANCE
BALANCE
DYNAMIC
BALANCE
BALANCE
DYNAMIC
BALANCE
DYNAMIC
BALANCE
DYNAMIC
DYNAMIC
BALANCE
DYNAMIC
DYNAMIC
BALANCE
DYNAMIC
DYNAMIC
DYNAMIC
BALANCE
DYNAMIC
DYNAMIC

Architecture is an art coalescing many disciplines. It is an art of the collective. Architects are the initiators of an ongoing dialogue between parties often carrying incompatible agendas. They all exist in a balance dynamic with the world.

Contending demands are sources of turbulence during the journey of those who seek to achieve poetry in their work. As the gatekeepers of values routinely neglected under the speculative impulses to capitalize on land, they remain the sole defenders of the quality of space for the end users. Issues of sustainability, efficiency, safety, and service are at the forefront of responsible practices committed to their own version of modernity. What is offered here, however, is an unusual take on sustainability. The most sustainable things in life are those things that you won't throw away because you love them too much. Without a doubt, to design spaces that people will love meets private interests as well. This goal requires more finesse than patchy decoration on a building envelope and fancy signage.

This balancing act calls for conviction on the necessity to reform the architect's participation to the development process. Their ideology needs revision to bring humanism to the center of their concern. In equal measure, those partaking in the making of the contemporary city are invited to be co-conspirators in a better world. This is no utopia. It is a programmatic attitude set to bring factual changes in the way architects do their work.

Architecture is a form of emotional and cultural activism. There is a sense of mission built into the building art. That intent fed our ancestors and can nurture our present and future with the update that our time requires. There is a reason for a nostalgia for the past, a reason that needs to be heard. Cognizant of the past, while being wholly projected into the future, architects dynamically inhabit these time zones to concoct a present designed to be inclusive of all human types, their distinct characters, opposing agendas, and differing views of the world, as well as their deep commonalities.

This is the program we are striving for in contemporary architecture, for our profession to focus on the creation of vibrant, sustaining communities of hope, through a deeper understanding of the emotional meanings we embody in our designs. Toward a reintroduction of a sense of the poetic, in balance with the rational, with the intention that this will help reestablish the relevancy of architecture to the public.

Folded

Wings

Developing land often equates to reconfiguring its role in the setting it is part of. Routinely it entails maximizing buildable area to increase the return on investment. In Silicon Valley this rings particularly true since its economy is magnetic for the global entrepreneurial appetite. Folded Wings, however, is structured around an alternative approach: the actual area of the building is unaltered from the existing. It is sited the same way as what was already there. Rather, what changes is its effectiveness in workplace community building and creating a resonant sense of place.

The design for Folded Wings angles the typical office bar at the midpoint of its footprint to outline an urban plaza that welcomes pedestrian circulation. The core and shell plan for workspace is left unchallenged but it delivers a tangible reward in the generated quality of this central public space. The angles used to bend the building and its proportion and to define the butterfly section are entirely intuitive. The parti in plan follows best practices in workplace planning, while at its edges, a controlled articulation of ins-and-outs confers significant visual interest thanks to the hypnotic interplay of light and shadow as sunrays hit the exterior surfaces. This two-story structure cantilevers those cutouts on the upper flooring, essentially becoming canopies shielding direct light to the floors below.

A freestanding structure with a canted canopy signals access to the two levels of parking below grade. Upon arrival from the parking garage, visitors encounter a butterfly theme embodied in a folded roof and a folded facade: folding is the leitmotif of this project. The multiplication of those roofs across the office buildings breaks the scale of the normative Silicon Valley anonymous office bar into visually comprehensible units that, when knitted together, add richness and texture to the massing. The symmetrical angling of two planes around an axis applied to the facade demonstrates that its repeated application yields architectural unity rather than a chaotic jumble of discrete design episodes. The effect is that of a small village surrounding an intimate and welcoming courtyard.

Although this is a speculative office building for technology companies and is occupied by two tenants, its overall appearance yields a form of humane modernism at the scale of the pedestrian. The recesses add texture and interest all around the building exterior, exhibiting only minor variations. The numerous overhangs on the first floor and the recesses on the second floor, as well as cost-effective solar control, allow for a significant amount of glass to be used while still making this a LEED-certified building.

Echoing the campus's various butterfly canopies, a very high-tech version of the butterfly marquee featuring fritted glass, specialized fittings, and a canted column mark the main entrance to the building. This compelling object of refined construction ushers the visitor to the experience of a most elegant glass box.

Sub-Urban Canyon

The fair weather of Silicon Valley affords the chance for this human-made suburban canyon to enliven the experience of working in Santa Clara. Here it takes the form of a landscaped street, which is activated by the communal activities that bring people together—from cafes to meeting rooms and a fitness center. Like a canyon, its lushness and intimacy are intended to draw you in, entice you to sit down with your laptop and start dreaming of the next innovation. The face of the canyon masks the four levels of a vast 3,400-car parking garage and becomes the other edge of an internal street, a park for public use. The elevated top of the garage is a large, landscaped oasis activated with soccer, softball, and tennis as well as strolling gardens and rich landscaped areas containing collaboration spaces, meeting pavilions, and secret gardens. These open to the public during the evenings and weekends, but are exclusive to office workers during weekdays.

The project wants to succeed as a generator of place at an iconic level and at an urban level. The Sub-Urban Canyon master plan steps out of the anonymity of the sprawl and promotes architectural identity through a pair of elliptical towers nested into a highly formalized hardscape. This duet of waffle-cone buildings aims to reshape the flat suburban skyline, to initiate change from a suburban landscape to one that embraces the beauty of human potential.

Oasis

Oasis was conceived as an iconic beacon for innovation and design, majestic and intimate at the same time. With a suspended tropical garden in the midst of futuristic building systems, the large expanse of glass and a multilevel enclosure match aspirations to leave a meaningful imprint for better in the world.

Purposefully totemic, the imagery of Oasis is conceived as a piece of technology itself. Its iconicity is justifiably technologically poignant. Sited on a tight urban parcel in Santa Clara, California, facing the Great America theme park, the project signals the inevitable shift in higher density and transit-oriented developments surfacing in Silicon Valley's anonymous, often uninspired landscape.

Intended as a prototype of tomorrow's workplace, Oasis's vision asserts itself at a distance to coax visitors into a world of urbanity and surprise. Set apart, and still a part of the city, the glimmering object rises in the sky on a transparent podium as the pinnacle of the immaterial—conferring lightness and friendliness while protecting the preciousness of ideas in formation in an industry constantly reinventing the future.

Oasis provocatively addresses Silicon Valley's lack of urban vibrancy and provides a clever solution to the issues of public and private access.

Here the ground plane offers up a completely public experience. A sequence of retail experiences activates the street, and as the ground curls into a canopy, a spacious public cafe captures the pedestrian flow. The sculptural and sinuous landscape is pierced strategically to filter light into the parking garage below.

In order to provide a compelling private experience, rewarding the office tower's workers with a unique experience, the Big Sky Garden was created on the ninth floor. This is an urban retreat, a place where people, an open-air café, and a grand environment come together; it is the oasis that gives the design its lyrical name. The Big Sky Garden is embedded in the platonic completeness of the elevated massing, yet set apart as an experience both within the building and in its relation to the object's surroundings. It is a persuasive version of an aspirational place, high above the valley floor, inaccessible yet alluring.

As an object of technology Oasis conveys desire. Big, yet accessible. Permeable and private. Public and intimate. Oasis is the poster child for the future of Silicon Valley.

Can a dream exceed the grasp of its intended inspiration?

Resonance

Over the last 20 years, in the San Francisco Bay Area, an enlightened cacophony of planners, city officials, architects, and the emergence of a strong YIMBY movement have begun to focus on building dense mixed-use developments around mass transit. Unfortunately, however, the Bay Area has yet to establish a regional transit system plan and a governing body that serve as stewards for the interests of future generations. In addition, housing has become a significant crisis, affecting the economic and social stability of the entire state of California.

Resonance sits at the nexus of these opportunities. An alluring dream condition exists on the windswept outer edges of a Silicon Valley city. Here lies a large tract of underutilized land, comprising one-story warehouses, parking lots, and the odd single-family house that is long past its prime. It sits at the confluence of almost every major Bay Area and local transit system. Our developer client asked, what if we designed with big aspirations? Resonance is designed to be inspiring, yet lovable, dense but at a humane scale, with a strong vision expressing the future of technology.

Over 80 acres, a chain of five pearls increases in intensity, culminating in a heroic and grand central plaza that connects BART, bus, subway, and light rail and high-speed rail systems. One emerges from this transit collection as a celebration of intentional urbanity. Four floors of housing, retail, restaurants, community education, and live/work spaces are activated by an expansive covered farmer's market and exhibition space, cultural centers, and a significant commitment to maker and artist spaces. In addition, an adjacent indoor arena holds live concerts and professional sports, providing powerful civic activation. Above this urban activation, 10 floors of office space alternating with housing provide a comprehensive development that embraces Live/Work/Play + Learn and Create.

With the intention to create a verdant place of natural abundance, the project layers access to roof gardens that embrace the paradox of public and private space, which allows both communities to thrive. Five vertical layers of landscape interconnect the five pearls to host a continuous pedestrian experience from grade all the way to the roof.

TRANSIT CENTER

Campus X

To start with a blank slate in a typical Silicon Valley suburban context, where all public and pedestrian life has historically been banished, is a daunting challenge. Campus X aspires to create an architecture that straddles the iconic and the humane in one design. It creates an architecture worthy of the scale and intensity of the innovation that occurs here, and, at the same time, it challenges Silicon Valley norms with a design that is permeable to the street, and invites public participation in a vibrantly place-centric way.

From an iconic standpoint, fluidity is a grand trait of the Internet. An architecture of fluidity makes a continuous space a virtue. Dynamic curvilinear surfaces travel space uninterrupted to stake out a three-dimensional environment with neither beginning nor end. It is an infinite loop without recursive stalling.

The three million square-foot mixed-use campus is made up of four V-shaped buildings. The edges of these buildings are sculpted to evoke the California cantilevers so distinctive of its mid-century heritage. Both endpoints of these linear buildings turned upon themselves are canted vertically and slanted horizontally, thus accentuating the structural audacity of these sharp edges. Pedestrians perceive these as "futuristic spaceships" of mythical proportions, wrapped into a world of convex surfaces catching all the vanishing points with its site limits. It is a spectacle of technology and engineering cleverness at the services of the memorable.

Form-making at this scale conjures awe. The massing eludes a closed reading of its volumes against the sky. And what transpires is a choreography of circulation. A web of pedestrian trajectories stakes out an intelligent system of paths that attends equally to function and leisure. To the clarity of its vertical and horizontal organization, the bold architectural presence captivates the collective attention of the visitors.

Campus X is unusually permeable to a public unconnected to the workforce. This porous public space invites gathering, encountering, and mutual viewing. Two enormous pedestrian ramps reach up from the street on the east side of the site, rising to converge toward its center. At the ground level, all spaces are activated through a 25-foot-high retail zone filled with product showrooms and amenity space capped by the glassed forms enclosing a multilevel edifice of offices.

Here, the humane and the iconic blend seamlessly. Sandwiched between the articulated topography of the ground plane and a futuristic skyline lies a pedestal starkly defined through a continuous disk serving both as canopy and visual marker. The spark of city life occurs. The social energy of past market life is revisited here through a string of architectural events—purposefully elegant to be magnetic destinations for visitors and workforce alike in a crescendo without apex. Each V-shaped building, evocative of a boomerang in plan, holds a vast private courtyard filled with amenities and outdoor opportunities, whereas, on the more public side, their convex nature generates a space of perpetual movement in its occupants. This approach embraces one of Silicon Valley's more complex paradoxes, that of providing both generous public and private space, wherein both set of participants feel treated fairly. This is in opposition to the normative practice of “fortress technology campuses” where the public is relegated to the periphery.

The forms of Campus X stem from these two qualitative considerations. Order, repetition, and pattern inform the design, bestowing identity. The outcome is an up-to-date version of the organic, crafting a unique skyline in the flat vastness of Silicon Valley. It is an architectural orchestration of the public and the private, constantly negotiating between the two, yet all conjuring to generate a pedestrian neighborhood scale.

The development of a skyline is a design theme as old as architecture itself. When reaching urban heights, orientation and a sense of identity for the community are the most visible outcome of that architectural ambition. Such understanding feeds the environmental vision of this proposed scheme. The Lake Merritt BART compound intentionally amps up its presence at street level and on the Bay Area horizon to sculpt a memorable massing on a physically low-shaped territory.

Its iconicity, however, is in its massing as it relates to the adjacent parcels and beyond. Two pairs of hexagonal drums, louvered and laid out horizontally on the long edges, set a confident presence on the land. Their plastic interpretation remains open. They could be read as innovative and futuristic shapes of the distinctive Bay Area Rapid Transit (BART) cars, or any other high-tech association provoked in the viewer. Regardless, while they are imposing at the level of the territory they are friendly to pedestrians, porous to human activity. This is a scheme organized to promote vibrancy on the ground where the urban energy finds physical resolution in a place propelling exchange, spontaneous gathering, resting in the outdoors, people-watching, and all those unscripted activities that make cities what they are.

Binary Harmonics

Driver of these assertive forms is the section. On a parking podium, 13 levels of office give shape to programmatic needs. A donut of retail and housing—half of which is dedicated to serve the low-income population—buffers the garage with the city edges. The functional parti is unambiguous and does respond to an area with an evolving demand as the East Bay's economic fate rises. In the experiential unfolding of this design there is a peak in destination: the roof garden on top. This is an aspirational place, that is a point of arrival in the discovery of the space as the visitors learn about the building. To get there, it requires intent, and the reward is a powerful vantage point from where to embrace the magnificent horizon of the San Francisco Bay Area.

The building enclosure offers a distinct striation of vertical and horizontal sunshades. They contribute to the forceful image that sets this project apart from its neighboring structures. On both the east and west ends the glass face is recessed back 20 feet to create a deep overhang blocking the western sun. Vertical glass fins provide further protection leaving the view clear. While the overall look of this proposal is rooted in high tech, its environmental systems are central to its sustainable performance. Its commitment to green standard is to be found in the innumerable design moves, often invisible, that make this a milestone within the construction practices of the area.

Architecture lasts when it latches onto the emotions of its community. When it is both evocative and invisible in its impeccable resolution of its functional demands. History is filled with milestones that have endured the test of time on those grounds. That is our long view.

Corten Ribbon

To embrace contemporary notions of sustainability is to consider renovating existing buildings rather than tearing them down. Embodied carbon is one of the most critical benefits. In Silicon Valley, this act is affectionately known as repositioning. Within this context, architects often encounter a significant challenge in addressing how to refresh buildings with little to no character, a curse endemic to large swaths of modernism. This is an opportunity to breathe life into emptiness.

The Corten Ribbon provides an iconic entrance experience visible from the public realm. This sculptural gateway to social exchange is a beacon. Functional architecture is turned into a lyrical object, lifting from the ground, to afford at every step and turn of landings countless opportunities for engaging views and celebrating the workforce as a vital community.

The Corten Ribbon was designed to create an edgy urban brand for the five-building Ygnacio Center Office Park in Walnut Creek, California. The sculptural, ribbon-like gateway was designed to modernize and reinvigorate the 50-year-old commercial office complex and maximize the buildings' potential as a bustling community space.

The perforated corten steel installation extends from the community building to the adjacent parking garage, creating a visually appealing social courtyard and a memorable entrance. The Ribbon's design concept echoes throughout the floorplan and project with angular shards, nonlinear corridors, and cove ceiling lighting.

A flexible linear courtyard serves as the social heart of this coworking community. Furnished with movable and permanent seating, benches, firepits, and six freestanding lyrical shades, the furnishings also emulate the Ribbon's geometric forms and enable active social engagement at different times of the day and evening.

There are a range of accommodated uses. Activated by a cafe/bar, the courtyard comes alive in the evenings and at lunchtime, harnessing the human drive to socialize. At the same time the space is also designed to encourage passive usage as a quiet place to work or relax, in between moments of more intense vibrancy.

Welcome

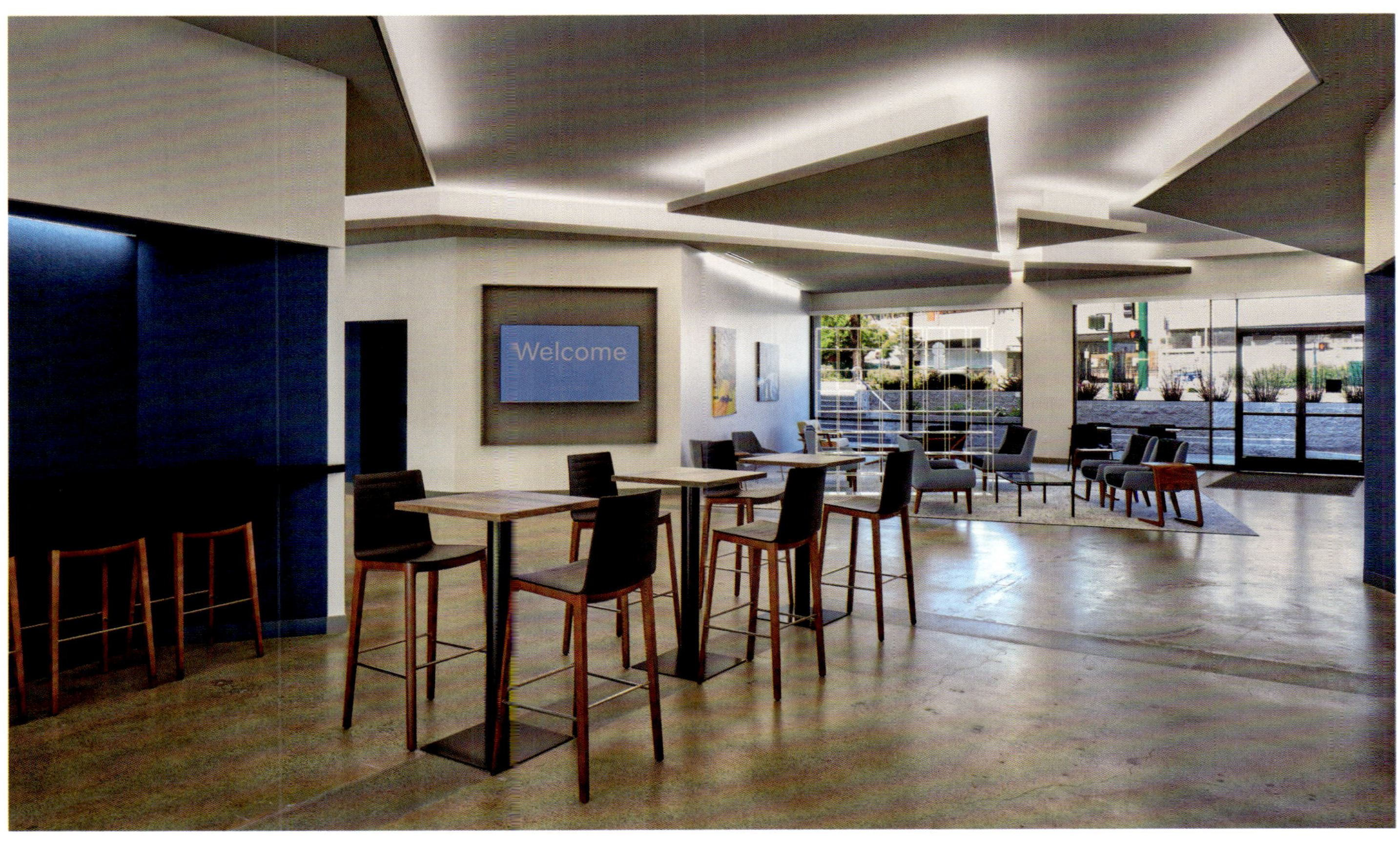
Welcome

Verdant
Sanctuary

Verdant Sanctuary expresses its embrace of nature through each design element: its natural setting, its wood and glass materiality, its dramatic roof design that echoes the shape of a bird's wings. There is a dynamic flow to these forms that pulls you along, giving you the feeling of an organic whole.

Through its various roof scales and levels, Verdant Sanctuary emphasizes a sense of horizontality. Projecting and receding volumes create a lively building envelope rather than a static flat facade. A generously scaled main entrance canopy is supported by structural elements that feature mass timber.

Utilizing passive sustainability strategies, the design uses large roof overhangs to shade the glass in the summer, and in the winter, when the sun is low, the large glass areas provide beneficial solar heat gain. The building is all-electric with PV panels for sustainable energy harvest and will feature a green roof as natural insulation.

This oasis is a pastoral break in a canyon of structures built on zero lot lines along the El Camino Real. A California xeriscape provides a buffer between the building and the street, harmonizing with surrounding buildings. Glass walls are so clear and unobstructed that the roofs seem to float, and nature surrounds you, providing a warm welcome and a place for creativity.

Dawn breaks over a verdant oasis
insects begin their morning rituals
of passing from plant to plant
starting a cycle of nourishment
that sustains an entire ecosystem.

A woman stretches out her arm
in a classic yoga pose
to greet the day in restorative contemplation.

While tea served in rough raku bowls
sparks inspiration
from nature's creative muse
in this most fertile sanctuary.

We started on a walk not really knowing where we were going just bored and looking needing to seize the morning air after a few days
the discordant intensity of urban life overwhelmed by the noise and with a desperate desire for cheaper space and safer schools
I love to walk in nature to breathe in the simple stillness of an empty meadow or to ascend the steep hills of San Francisco
only a dull sameness of perfect lawns large houses flat sidewalks that no one walks on that lead to nowhere after a
act of rebellion won't change anything We walked past vast parking lots that buffer big boxes of shopping for
walking reminding ourselves it would be time to turn back soon or we would miss a promised lunch We
just letting you know you are here a slowly rising road gave us space for decompression from ...
but human scaled made back from a time when the solid earth mattered and things were made
The buildings were eclectic each with its own personality each with its own stories waiting
different architects ..... different hands The campus rambled in the most delightful way
nature things moved flowing like an ancient hill town with wisdom hidden in the
earth That this and every part of the earth is sacred the buildings were new
wide range of aesthetic paradoxes chaotic + ordered dynamic +
kindness The buildings were lovable which in turn meant loved
passes on to the next generation you could feel the human
in balance with a sweet thoughtfulness rigor and
the framework the history of this place provoking a
context nothing seemed static in the
there seemed to be space and agency
new patina of creative tension

catching up with friends their house was located in an unremarkable suburb south of a large midwestern town it seemed a rejection of
on the third day our friends suggested "there is a group of unusual buildings at the community college" it was a lifeline ... an escape
and Tuscany where every moment is a revelation Here there was less than chaos a plastic banality with an absence of decay
while the sameness overwhelms you tempted to scream, you realize that aside from the momentary disruption this little
manufactured goods a utopian nightmare of Bauhaus ordinariness played out for the mass consumer We kept
found the road there was a simple sign an elegant hint of minimalist rigor ... it was not selling you something
suburban world When we arrived This was no ordinary place The first moment an entry gate grand
by hand with care It pulled you in it welcomed you it threw open its heart with warmth and love
inside you could imagine sitting all day absorbing the collective knowledge of humankind
following the course of the land in a deliberately expressive yet reverent balance with
dark shadows waiting to be revealed Here you could feel the deep energy of the
but seemed like they could have been there for a millennium embracing a
modest hard + soft complex + simple providing abundance warmth
and cared for and ultimately renewed with passion when that love
touch everywhere in an explosion of personalities but always
discipline even what "graffiti" was offered respected
curiosity about defining what that means in this
dappled light of an old grove of oak trees
to for an evolution for change to add a
and humanity

CULTURAL VIBRANCY

We are all, at a fundamental level, dreamers. Dreams can deeply influence our destinies, aspirations, and goals. As architects, we are some of the world's grandest dreamers, and this comes in no small part from the sheer range of scales at which we dream—from the room to the building, the city, and the region. At all of these scales we create a context for the fertile workings of life. We, in essence, design for people, to give space for their dreams, through our creativity and imagination.

We strive to create buildings and cities that have a high degree of cultural activity, authenticity, and a strong sense of community. We desire an engaged population that not only loves their environment but also participates in its creation and ongoing evolution. The extension of which means they feel responsible for its maintenance and improvement, and are inspired and empowered to infuse it with their cultural and artistic energy. They create traditions and rituals which carry this collective effort forward to successive generations. Ideally this vibrancy extends across the full range of socioeconomic strata so that everyone participates and enjoys these benefits. If they are successful, they will extend this caring sense of community beyond the physical environment toward caring for each other's well-being, because they sense how each of us contributes to the success of our communities.

If we follow this dream back into the architectural profession, our goal might be seen as helping to create vibrancy. Let me suggest a pairing—Cultural Vibrancy. This is something more than default "energetic" architectural vibrancy, and in this case "culture" is meant to be the arts and their related customs, traditions, and values. It is the dynamic relationship between expressive forms of culture and it is people themselves that make this concept thrive.

The richness of Cultural Vibrancy might be summed up as the relationship between three values: Depth + Range + Engagement. Here, depth relates to the quality of an experience, how moving it is, how well the program serves the population who uses it, how thoughtfully it was designed. This is the area where the architect and designer have the greatest impact. The range of cultural vibrancy depends on how wide and inclusive the groups served by architecture are. The essential ingredients of range are people, objects, and the design community. The wider the range of people served, the greater vibrancy there will be within the community, which, by result, will be healthier and more sustainable.

Engagement is the direct personal interactions, both passive and active, you might have with others and the community at large. Active forms include making things like art or music, participating in governance of the maintenance of your neighborhood or buying a new bench for the community to enjoy. If you don't feel personally engaged with your community, whether it is your street, your neighborhood or the vast community of humankind, you will become isolated.

Cultural Vibrancy leads to places that have emotional meaning. It is emotional meaning that aids in reconnecting the inner and outer dimensions of our world. When rigor and heart are balanced, they infuse the built environment with a sense of place.

Andromeda Reimagined

Andromeda Reimagined, a sanctuary in the Deep Playa of the Nevada desert during Burning Man, is a homage to women both heroic and sublime. Following the Burning Man 2019 theme of "Metamorphosis," the five-sided pyramid takes the original Greek tale of Andromeda—saved by Perseus from a death sentence before attaining celestial immortality—and reimagines Andromeda as a strong, independent woman who saves herself with the help of her supportive community.

Five oval panels welcome participants who enter looking for respite. On the first panel, they can read in the poem, entitled "How Brightly," about the limitless potential of our relationship to the universe. It's surrounded by four Allegory panels, painted by Mary Graham, depicting the reimagined narrative. In the first, Andromeda is confronted with the chains holding her back. In the second, she struggles with her inner demons. In the third, her community comes to support her and she comes to terms with her strengths and weaknesses. In the fourth panel, Andromeda finds her bliss and joins the stars in the night sky, illuminating our dreams.

An eight-foot-high, 2,000-pound concrete sculpture, by artist Mischell Phoenix Riley, called "Freedom and Awaken" anchors the center of the site, reflecting the theme from an oceanic perspective.

Casting whimsical patterns onto the desert floor, the CNC patterns invite visitors to examine where they fall in the gendered spectrum of the loosely borrowed Jungian concept of Anima-Animus. The geometric white patterns reflect a more typically male perspective of linear, logical, and mathematical elements, while the fluid blue patterns are more female, sensuous, and intuitive. Both are strong and pretty, and beyond coexisting, they work in harmony with each other, which ultimately expresses a provocation to embrace this paradox, rather than to resolve it.

The playful structure itself relates to the infinite romantic potential of the stars in the sky—specifically the Andromeda constellation.

YOUR LIFE
IS NOT MEASURED BY
HOW BRIGHTLY
YOU MIGHT SHINE
FOR ONE GLORIOUS MOMENT
AS THE SUN
BUT RATHER
IN HOW BEAUTIFULLY
YOU ADD
YOUR LIGHT
TO THE UNIVERSE
OF STARS
IN THE EVENING SKY
C.C.M.

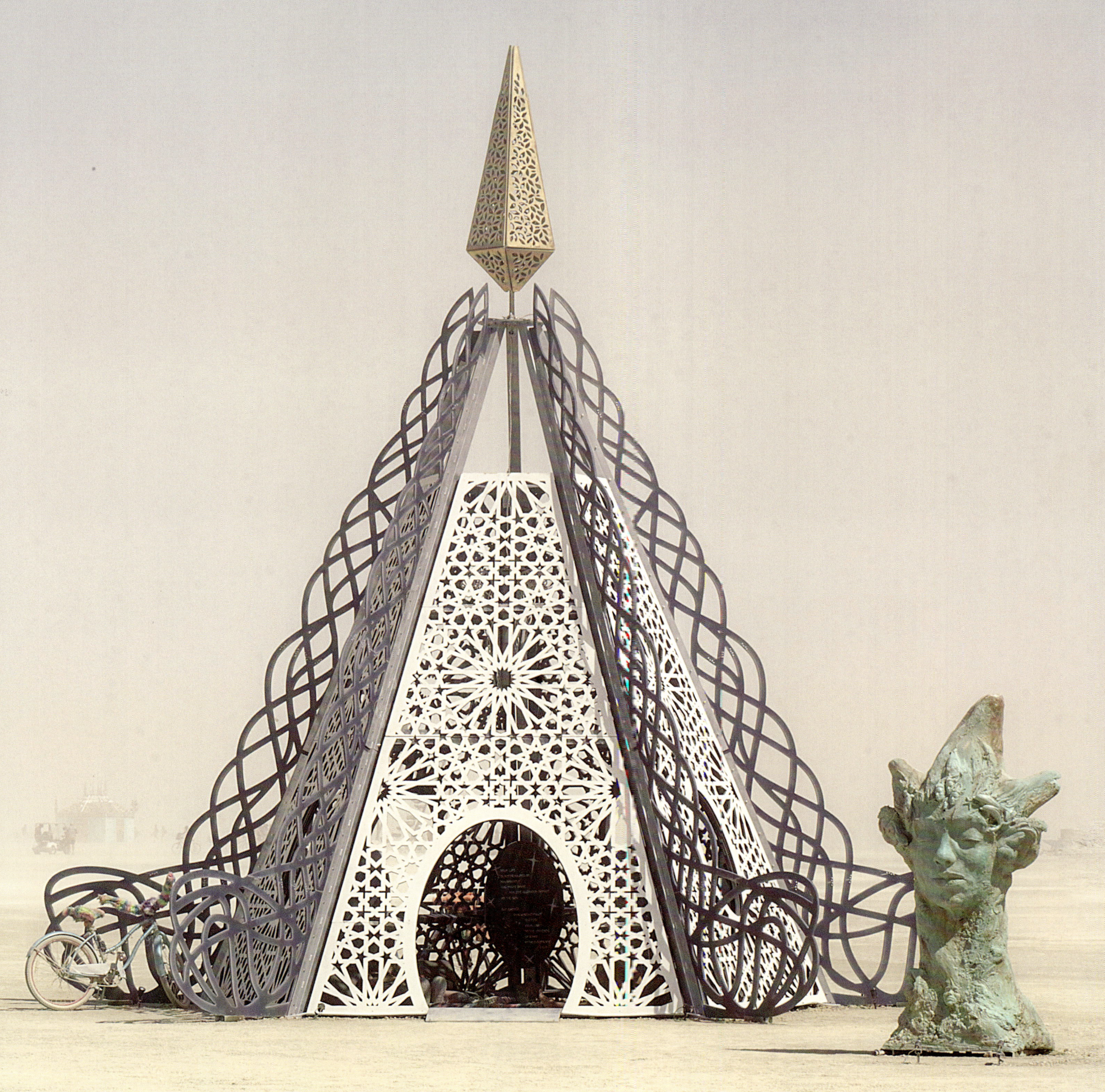

Museum of No Spectators

Out near the dusty perimeter of Black Rock City lies a different kind of museum. This intriguing and mysterious building with its unusually shaped galleries appears to be part machine, part creature, part abstract and surrealistic form. It presents as a blank slate, with an expansive exterior, and letters spelling Museum of No Spectators hovering above. Its dynamic shapes emerge as otherworldly yet grounded.

The Museum of No Spectators (MoNS) emphasizes inclusivity, in line with the wholly participatory nature of Burning Man culture. It creates a space for everyone to make art and become an exhibiting artist. With art continuing to develop during the Burning Man event week, "Burners" self-express by bringing original art, adding to or subtracting from existing pieces, or creating their own in this decommodified space using art materials provided by the museum.

The visitor is no longer a consumer but someone entering a thoroughly inclusive space where the creative process is a key element in how the art is shared with others—an inherently decommodifying experience. Reflecting on Banksy's provocative statement about museum commodification "exit through the gift shop," in the MoNS one enters through the Gifting Shop. We have fundamentally changed the use of the word "shop" to mean "to make" instead of "to buy." The museum encourages visitors to make a gift of art before proceeding into the main exhibition space. A team of Artists in Residence take people through the ritual of creating art, by providing instruction and materials. MoNS also changed the use of the word "gift" from a noun to a verb, "Gifting," gifting 5,000 photographs and 3,000 pieces of jewelry. Throughout the event, more than 60 artists of 14 nationalities posted artwork and 53% of the artists were BIPOC.

The 1,400-square-foot structure built of tube steel framing and aluminum wall panels emerged from the desert after 10 days of building by a team of 40 volunteers. The main museum comprises eight galleries, each dedicated to a different theme—Social Justice: Truth, Lies, and Reconciliation; Snark: Tell It Like It Is—With a Wry Smile; Sparkle Pony: Whimsy, Love, and Joy; Wisdom: Paradox, Balance, and Transcendence; Discovery/Identity/Epiphany: Emergence and Transformation; Into the Darkness: Mystery and Vortex; The Future: Community, Kindness, and Forgiveness; Earth and Sustainability: The Ethereal Landscape.

RECUERDOS
PAST, PRESENT + FUTURE

On the dusty edges of a distant playa an inclusive museum tempts you to embrace community and kindness through participatory art

Museum of
No Spectators

Museum of
No Spectators

BLESSING
GOD IS KING

The Golden Cage

The rich and lyrical symbolism of Metamorphoses was the theme for the 2019 Burning Man event. Located at the geographic center of Black Rock City, the pavilion is the symbolic and cultural focus of the event. For seven days a wooden sculpture of The Man stands atop a base that is designed specifically for the event. On the eighth day the entire structure is burned in an operatic ritual of fire and artistry.

For many, metamorphosis begins with a journey. In the realm of humankind, most journeys begin with a destination. There is a fixed plan, a schedule, an itinerary; we move at a logical pace. If history has taught us anything, however, it is that true change and transformation follow a path of mystery and ambiguity. As such, they will most certainly not follow a linear path, and the outcome can be intensely unpredictable.

This design suggests an experience symbolizing the nature of Metamorphoses, which allows us to celebrate those who have made that journey, and those who are about to embark. Five concepts are interwoven to create the central structure, loosely based on Ovid's tales.

The first takes the form of two heroic wings suggestive of flight, but not exactly the pure form of a butterfly. There is ambiguity; it could be a bird, or the wings of Icarus, a symbol of Man's passion and arrogance.

The second is expressed by a large blue sphere, symbolizing the earth and all the potential our time on this planet represents.

The third, the figure of two large arms that seem to offer up the globe to the heavens, is an adaptation of Ovid's dark tale of Apollo pursuing Daphne with the intention of raping her. In our transformative version, these hands now allude to a regreening of the earth, rather than its current course of self-destruction, giving hope for a better planet.

The fourth is the Golden Cage surrounding the Man, representing the internal and external forces that keep us from realizing our potential as human beings.

The last concept involves the power of the human heart. At the top of the globe, right under the Man, is a platform with an inlaid heart-shaped one-way mirror. Participants who get on their knees and look intensely into that heart can see the whole universe. This is your universe, this your heart, and you know, in that moment, this is where you belong.

This is your universe,
this your heart, and you know,
in that moment, this is where you belong.

Human

Convergence

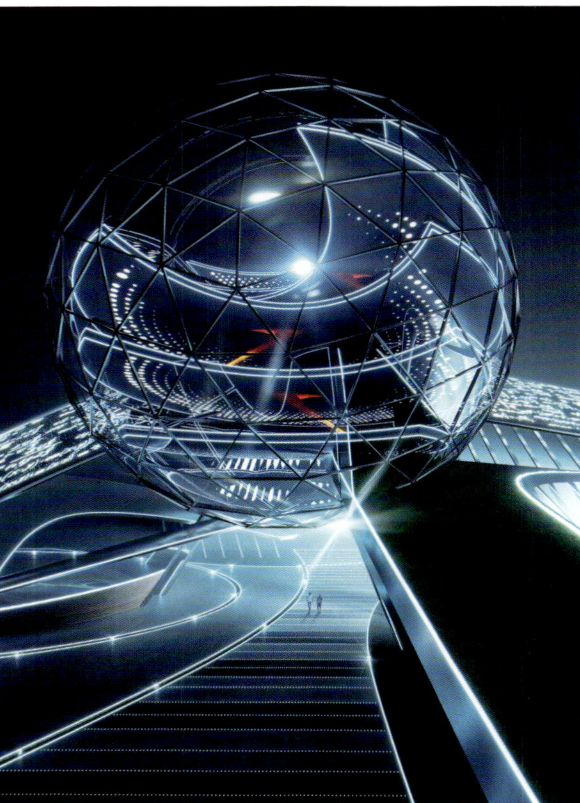

Open-ended and inherently inclusive, Human Convergence is an architectural invitation to congregate. Its transformational presence is a confident gesture broadcasting to the world Silicon Valley's paramount role in harnessing human talent under enlightened entrepreneurship.

A pliable framework of potential uses, this architectural ensemble is a park, a space to gather, a locus of authentic exchange, a lyrical place to dream the impossible, a catalyst for individual and collective inspiration, a setting to be inhabited as communal needs arise.

Icons locate place and mark the memorable. The eastern arc represents a phase when societies rooted in religion were slowly discovering science and its consequences. Life was organized in accord with Nature, using technology organic with the environment and prompting a coherent culture in balance.

In traveling the full length of the western portion of the site, the arc contains the Agora and the Sphere facing the Guadalupe River. The former contains cafes, art installations, and areas for spontaneous performances. The latter, floating in space, offers a place for people to come together and enjoy art, explore scientific discoveries, and hone their own craft in making things. It is an interactive museum for the reconciliation of these three realms. The "Gallery of Aspiration" occupies the globe's summit, where the unlimited potential of the self is sensed emotionally. Looking at the surrounding views, this expansive sense of the future is reinforced.

This project both landmarks the present and expresses the convergence of Nature, culture, and technology to create a more humane future. It brings diverse groups of people together as better human beings in a harmonious way built on a common vision, where compassion for "otherness" is imbued with renewed humanity.

The Portal

Might the future of technology help us rediscover what it means to be human?

Symbols are potent identifiers of a world, city, culture, or era. They often exemplify the best aspects of the people they represent, both in the ways that a culture identifies itself and in defining how the world sees that culture. The most profound symbols are those that move beyond a landmark's strong formal qualities to be active participants in transformation.

The Portal represents a unique and rare opportunity to offer a deeply immersive and participative experience that will be a platform to not only symbolize and define but also facilitate the co-creation of a new era for humanity. On the broadest level, the project's mission is to demonstrate, test, and experiment with agency for change. The Portal creates a platform to engage the world about the human condition, to foster a sense of community, to develop the fundamental need for humanity to care about each other, and, as result, to cocreate solutions to the wide range of problems the world faces.

This project embraces the unprecedented opportunity of the Metaverse and the intersection of virtual and physical realms. It shapes the future on a global scale, leveraging this fusion to redefine experiences and foster transformative change.

The Portal is a transportation hub with physical spaces for a conference center, hotel, experience center with retail and restaurants, arboretum, viewing space, and residential units.

Visitors are transported to different worlds (the Metaverse) via personalized journeys within the immersive Portal. The Portal's transportive experiences are achieved through physical and virtual layers. Each layer is designed to evolve and adapt, absorbing new content, new technology, and even new purpose.

The building concept is for the Portal to act as a living laboratory for emerging technologies. In the space between the inner and outer walls there is room for a variety of infrastructure. Water is recycled locally to feed irrigation and central cooling plants. An energy vault uses compressed air and gravity energy storage. A food wall recycles food waste and generates healthy soil, and includes traditional systems and state-of-the-art hydroponics.

Demonstrated throughout the project are the building's high-performance design concepts. The building envelope will incorporate passive house design standards for insulation, a vented skin, and a naturally vented interior volume with precooling from earth tubes. The systems will include radiant tempered slab and localized evaporative cooling for passive temperature control—combined with the large volume, a cool, comfortable environment will be maintained.

The Portal is an active catalyst for the transformation of generations of visitors. A major presence in the Metaverse, it is an immersive storytelling experience and an inspiring educational platform that articulates the potential of sustainable urban living. It offers a unique journey into future communities, transforming visitors into informed advocates for a global life, work, and play ethos.

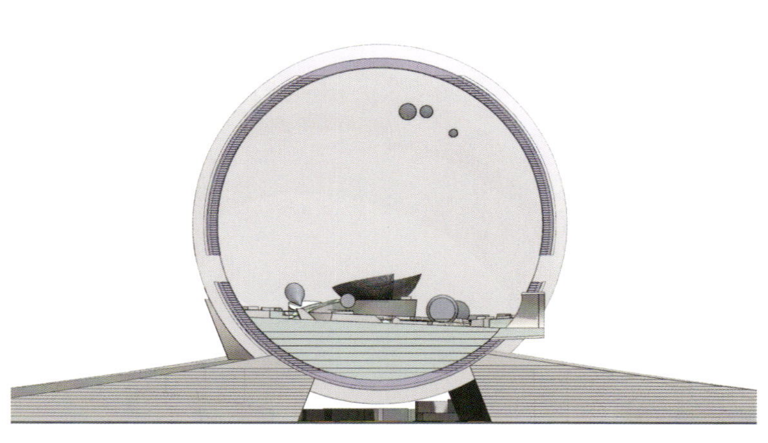

IoT
Internet of Things

ADVOCACY
ADVOCACY
ADVOCACY
ADVOCACY
ADVOCACY
ADVOCACY
ADVOCACY
ADVOCACY
ADVOCACY
ADVOCACY
ADVOCACY
ADVOCACY
ADVOCACY
ADVOCACY
ADVOCACY
ADVOCACY
ADVOCACY
ADVOCACY
ADVOCACY
ADVOCACY
ADVOCACY
ADVOCACY
ADVOCACY
ADVOCACY
ADVOCACY
ADVOCACY
ADVOCACY
ADVOCACY
ADVOCACY
ADVOCACY
ADVOCACY
ADVOCACY
ADVOCACY
ADVOCACY
ADVOCACY
ADVOCACY
ADVOCACY
ADVOCACY
ADVOCACY
ADVOCACY
ADVOCACY

We all respond to the conditions of our time—whether consciously or not—by adding to or subtracting from an apparent sense of progress. At this moment, modern architecture is at a critical crossroads, where it needs to admit to its past transgressions, its current public alienation, while also celebrating the progress it has nurtured. In learning from these, architecture has to move forward thoughtfully and perhaps radically to truly fulfill its potential to be of service to and inspire humanity.

I'm advocating for a fundamental change in the way architects design, with the intention of rebalancing Modernism toward an architecture of emotional abundance, rather than its current singular focus on an architecture of ideas and abstraction. This involves rebalancing the role of emotional meaning in design intent, as well as evaluating the impact of what we create on the public at large. I'm responding to the notion that architecture has disengaged with society and is losing its cultural relevance. A rebalancing should be seen as an additive approach, welcoming emotional meaning back into our design intent.

Emotional meaning is not the sole foundation of design, but its absence strips architecture of its essence. It serves as the elusive core that connects the act of building to the sublimation of the self—a fusion of pleasure, bliss, and a sense of belonging. The body responds to an artifact that is designed with intent to transcend mere functional requirements. Such designs forge a connection that unites the individual fragments of humanity into a cohesive whole.

Emotional meaning supplies architects with the capacity to discern the priceless against the dispensable. It helps to reestablish the general public's trust and affection toward architects. It constitutes an opportunity to reengage clients with the value of architecture. It resets the architect's outlook to design with people and art as indissoluble essentials of architecture.

Nostalgia Commercialism Iconicity
Superficiality Authenticity

Within a notion of the ascendancy of emotional meaning in the design of architecture, there are five critical concepts we must come to terms with, and thoughtfully bear in mind. These issues will exist in any effort to design; what is important is to optimize the degree to which they do exist, to create the best possible outcome.

What does an ideal architecture of abundance look like?
It would involve a change in intentions, rather than a specific visual reference.

If we look over the past 100 years, austere and minimalistic architectures have been revered for their poetry and their power. Far less frequently are buildings praised for their sweetness, their grace, or how lovable they are. In a culture that tends to favor attributes associated with masculinity, a whole range of expressions has been repressed.

To go further we should discuss what makes for "lovable" architectures. Whether beautiful, caring, humane, or comforting, the definition of "lovable" encompasses a whole range of interpretations—delightfully subjective, but all crucial to understand in building a more equitable and expressive future. An architecture of emotional abundance is less a case of defining what "lovable" is as a singular style, but rather in offering the provocation, "what would lovable mean to the individual architect?" I would much rather see what a million designers would create with a lovable intention.

In order to return a sense of humanity to design, we advocate for a rebalancing of modernism with emotional meaning and poetic design.

Our advocacy has taken seven paths.

How We Advocate:

COMMENT 30

THE ARCHITECT'S NEWSPAPER MARCH 25, 2015

COMMENT> PIERLUIGI SERRAINO AND JOHN MARX

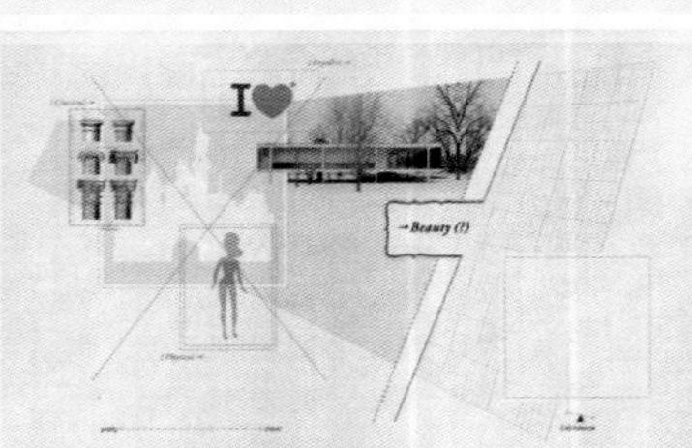

JEREMY MENDE

Emotional Meaning: The Intangible of Architecture

SETTING THE STAGE

Remember the last time you changed your route to stop and visit a particular building? You may have wanted to see it for some time; perhaps it was a curiosity or a tribute to your student days. Imagine you are there, entering the realm of its presence with all the particularities of your own life. That architecture is inevitable, substantive, impactful, consequential, and undeniably timeless. Still, in its beauty, the construction is a mute messenger of the larger order of things that you sense within, but are unable to declare. This artifact is the resonance chamber of all that is uncontainable within you. What you are seeing, occupying, savoring—in a word experiencing—is emotionally meaningful. We hold this to be a primary aspiration in the making of architecture. Emotional meaning aids in reconnecting the inner and outer dimensions of our world.

When avant-garde modernists chose to prize reason over emotion, architecture detached itself from the world it was meant to improve. The cold rationality of performance and concept-based design left out the intangibles that make us human. Estrangement followed.

Design without rigor inexorably turns capricious. On the other hand, design without heart lays out urban cemeteries. When rigor and heart are balanced, they infuse the city fabric with a sense of place. Bonding and belonging ensue. Emotional meaning in architecture occurs when the elements or the character of a space arouse an emotional response in the user that is meaningful, significant, and enduring.

In an attempt to understand the structural relationship between architecture and people, can emotions be conceived as a cognitive basis for design rather than being hastily dismissed as personal opinions?

It is within reason to say that few members of the public experience an emotional connection to today's architecture. Design as problem solving often neglected this aspect, producing an ecosystem out of balance and fraught with undesirable consequences. The ascetic restraint of Miesian descent brought, and still brings, chilling austerity to the global urban imagery. Broadly speaking, current design tends to fall into two trends: sanitized glass-boxes rooted in a mid-century modern revival or Wild West formalism with fashionable architecture on stylistic overload. Either way, we are facing a particularly aggressive challenge on the emotional meaning front. Pervasive computing has enabled reckless self-indulgence from those architects married to innovation no matter what, whose formal language has imploded under the pressure of originality at all cost. Our heads are spinning between bombastic statements about fantasies of mass-customization and the sadistic warping of unitized systems to adapt to predetermined forms, the wilder the better. Both camps operate without a working understanding of the role of emotional meaning in architecture.

WHERE WE WERE. WHERE WE ARE.

The 20th century saw the hard sciences triumphant. Yet something went profoundly wrong. Calculus proved to be a defective instrument in solving the intractable problems pertaining to the broader human equation. Urban blight, one of the copious global scars of relentless industrialization, is the most discernible outcome of an engineering logic left unchecked. It is ubiquitous, inevitable, and of overwhelming magnitude. It stands as the deformed child of the unhappy union between mathematical reasoning operating on autopilot and design processes rooted in declarative procedures with no human insight. Obsession with problem solving, on material "honesty," on the social overpowering the formal, and on the fetishizing of technology for technology's sake has lead to the general public's alienation from architecture.

Thinking took over from feeling. The humanities got the short end of the stick. It would be all well and good if individuals were machines, but we know that to be untrue. Still we have yet to bear witness to a change in outlook. It is our contention that emotion links environments to their users and is fundamental to the architectural experience. Its role in architectural discourse is not just desirable, but necessary, as it would greatly expand the capacity of architects to symbolically reach the people they claim to design for. As buildings over time undergo changes in how they embody programmatic requirements, they remain vehicles for the renewal of emotional meaning. While a ubiquitous response, emotion's specific realization is anything but universal. It differs in every person. The fact that two individuals can experience opposite emotional meaning in the same structure establishes a common ground between them even in the face of this polarity.

Where did the resistance to emotions as a design factor come from? Terminology might have something to do with this discursive impasse. Some words, like beauty, can be so historically charged that their association with what are held as outmoded notions or past memories must be erased in the formative processes of new generations. Today we hear that customers have turned into "guests," and employees are "dismissed" as opposed to being unceremoniously fired. What semantic transformations have "emotions" undergone in the patois of the highbrow crowd of the past 40 years? Given the secular nature of 20th century culture and beyond, emotions are perilously evocative of faded romanticism, signposts of irrelevant concerns to what today's gatekeepers of architectural discourse deem to be currency. They dispose of emotions as annoying, sentimental yearnings unsuitable to the blueprint of cultural and societal reformation that the promoters of modern and post-modern architecture have endorsed. Our critics offer an array of alternative idioms to talk effectively about the same notion. A glaring example is the tragic anonymity of Silicon Valley. As visitors, we cannot help wondering what the root cause is for the inverse relationship between unparalleled financial wealth and the deterioration of the urban condition in the same territory. Design platitude is all around us. It is the malaise of our time and exclusively of our own making.

Form-making by itself is an empty exercise, negating the qualitative function of architecture in human existence. Self-expression, on the other hand, is the filtering of circumstances and contingency through the sensibility of an individual, resonating with the socio-physical character of the site. Rationality alone cannot resolve the conflicts between these two seemingly opposite points of view. Hyper-focus on the physical metrics of the human body, e.g. design based on human scale handbooks, or equation-based design, e.g. parametric architecture, are likely shortcuts to a space of collective alienation.

A WAY FORWARD

Emotional meaning supplies architects with the capacity to discern the priceless against the dispensable. Bringing it back into the broader dialog is especially useful given how participatory design has taken renewed hold as we go deep into the 21st century. Finally, the faceless stakeholders get their seat at the design table sharing the entries until now in the hands of financial and program driven clients. Emotional meaning will add its weight into the balance mix to cater long-term to the community in factual ways.

Emotional Meaning matters now for the following reasons:

It helps to re-establish the general public's trust and affection toward architects.

It constitutes an opportunity to reengage clients to the value of architecture.

It resets the architect's outlook to design with people and art as in dissoluble essentials of architecture.

Ever cognizant of the failures of the past—like the use of emotions for the opportunistic to legitimize their designs and populate the environment with the unsightly—a starting list would include the following four offenders, guilty of crowding the arena of our sedated perception:

The *Nostalgic*: a sentimental longing for a past period, which is romanticized through the artistic artifacts of that era. The fallacy of nostalgia is that when the conditions that produced the artifacts no longer exist and the human condition has progressed from that point in time, this past loses its relevance and can no longer be credibly recreated.

The *Superficial*: the cult of the physique. The superficial is still the focus of normative notions of beauty. Appearance over content is the quintessential antinomy of this ideal. Rather than being a popularity contest, architecture aims at longer-term values.

The *Commercial*: unrestrained consumerism and transient gratification. When the primary purpose of the design of an object is to pander to the base instincts of a group in order to maximize sales, the end result is most often products that are shallow and short-lived.

The *Inauthentic*: something that is not of its time; something that is untrue to the conditions and nature of its time, material, or technology; something that appears to be what it is not.

Emotional meaning alone is not the basis of design; but its absence renders architecture without merit. It is the inscrutable raison d'être that links the act of building to the sublimation of the inner self; a mixture of pleasure, bliss, and rootedness. The physiology of the body starts registering the presence of an artifact designed with intent to go beyond the circumstantial practicalities of the program. It is intelligible in its nuanced aspirations, while providing the bond to hold the personal blocks that form the whole of humanity. Emotional meaning stirs catharsis to the collective and that unfathomable togetherness that resets individuals' unwavering commitment to kinship. This is territory foreign to rational planning, the quicksand of engineering analysis.

This reflection is presented to jumpstart a conversation within the architecture community. In weaving emotions back into the evaluation criteria, we are advocating for a disciplined practice of design where the metaphysical layer that always existed in architecture, whether in religious or secular centuries, can find an explicit and sustainable resolution into a material arrangement that speaks to the concerns and emotional bandwidth of 21st century inhabitants. In pursuing a much tighter fit than ever before between form and emotion, architects can once again exercise their capacity to steer society toward the realization of their current understanding of citizenship, well-being, and healthy participation of community members into the public realm.

JOHN MARX AND PIERLUIGI SERRAINO ARE AUTHORS AND ARCHITECTS WHO LIVE IN THE BAY AREA.

The Architect's Newspaper, March 2015

1 Emotional Meaning

An Initial Query

Emotional meaning alone is not the basis of design; but its absence renders architecture without merit. It is the inscrutable raison d'être that links the act of building to the sublimation of the inner self; a mixture of pleasure, bliss, and rootedness. The physiology of the body starts registering the presence of an artifact designed with intent to go beyond the circumstantial practicalities of the program. It is intelligible in its nuanced aspirations, while providing the bond to hold the personal blocks that form the whole of humanity. Emotional meaning stirs catharsis in the collective and that unfathomable togetherness that resets individuals' unwavering commitment to kinship. This is territory foreign to rational planning, the quicksand of engineering analysis.

Venice Biennale 2016

Visual poems and emotional meaning

By default architecture implies an intense commitment to being in the world. It has physical extension; it involves sequencings; and it constitutes the autobiographical imprint in material substance of its creator. In brief, it resides in Time, Space, Existence.

The *9[+3] Conversations* is a visual-textual artwork dealing with the broader philosophical choices architects make in their longing for meaningful space. 9 are pictorial poems illustrating an architectural design philosophy. [+3] are the existential premises journaling the uniquely personal itinerary of those individuals embracing architecture as a life project: the why (Epiphany), one's place in the order of things (Avocation), and the challenged navigation of one's own choices in life (Existence). The rebus is the rhetorical device both groupings share within the artwork. As an ensemble, they invite viewers to decode, interpret, connect, reflect. Each poem intersects the Visual (V), the Textual (T), and the Work (W), three areas encompassed in a living philosophy.

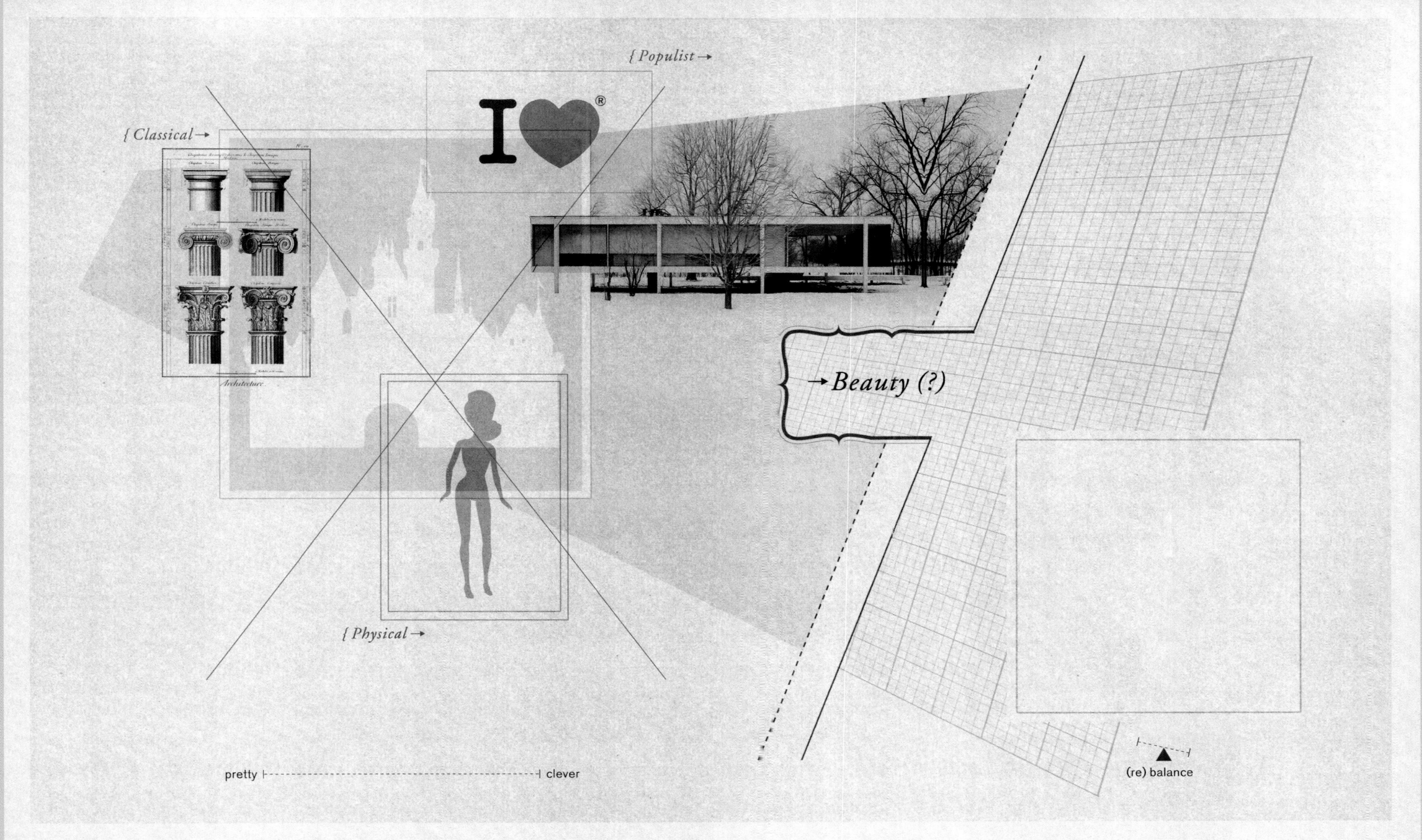

Emotional meaning equips architects with the ability to distinguish the invaluable from the trivial. It plays a vital role in restoring the public's trust and admiration for architects, offering an opportunity to reconnect clients with the true value of architecture. It shifts the architect's perspective, emphasizing the inseparable bond between people and art as foundational to design. Embracing the importance of emotional meaning in architecture brings forth five critical concepts that must be acknowledged and thoughtfully considered. These elements will always influence the design process, but the key lies in optimizing their presence to achieve the most impactful and meaningful outcomes.

Nostalgia
Commercialism
Iconicity
Superficiality
Authenticity

2 Second Century Modernism

Venice Biennale, 2018

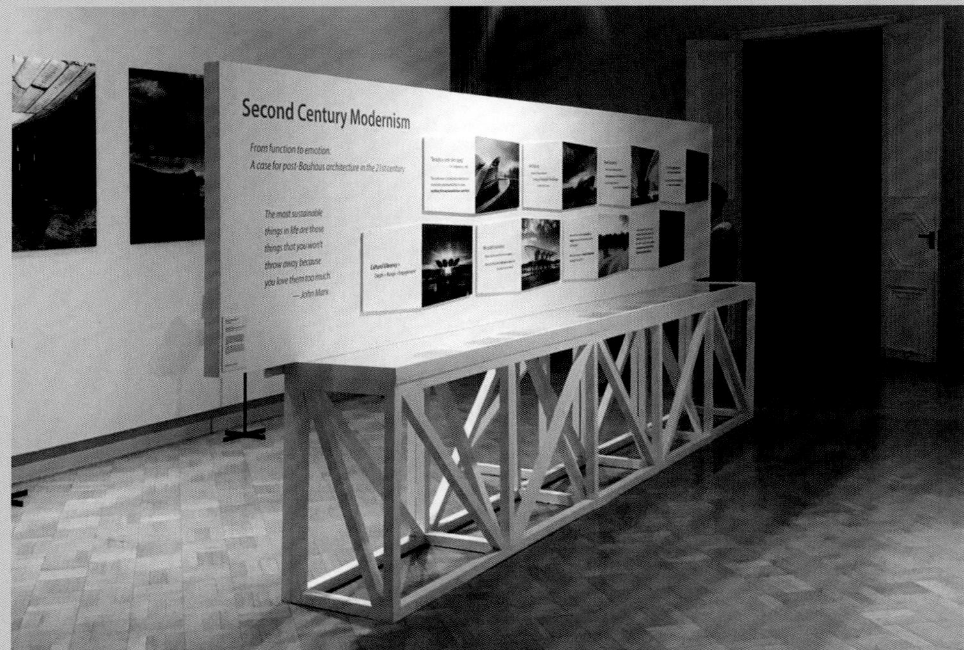

Public Architecture—Future for Europe, The Schusev State Museum of Architecture, Moscow, 2020

Second Century Modernism fosters an architecture of abundance, richness, and community by prioritizing Emotional Meaning, rebalancing the design process to integrate rationality with intuition, and adopting a "Less + More" philosophy that broadens and harmonizes cultural values in our spaces. It invites you to embrace the paradoxical nature of human existence.

3 The Absurdity of Beauty

"The Absurdity of Beauty: Rebalancing the Modernist Narrative" challenges the current philosophies of modernism and posits how these discussions can inspire a new era of urbanism and abundance.

Do buildings and environments create emotional meaning? If we assume that they do, how can we do a better job of designing forms and spaces that can resonate emotionally with the public?

The publication calls for a transformative shift in the way architects design, aiming to complement modernism's current emphasis on abstraction and ideas with a focus on emotional abundance. By elevating the importance of emotional meaning we also consider the broader impact of architecture on the public.

Developed with *The Architectural Review*, the volume includes contributions by Paul Finch, John Marx, Pierluigi Serraino, and Catherine Slessor.

“Burning Man encourages you to embrace Community and Kindness, through Participatory Art”

4 Cultural Vibrancy

Burning Man

Burning Man is not a laboratory to simply "understand placemaking," it is not an "architecturally" rich environment in the normative formal sense we use in our profession, but in spite of this, and in some ways because of this, a city of 70,000 people build their own vibrancy, in the most deeply authentic way possible, with the work of their own hands.

5 Creative Communities

Developing emerging communities through Culture

A Creative Community is a community whose shared value system revolves around the attraction of participatory art, of embracing and sharing self-expression, of empowering and unlocking the inherent creative and imaginative spirit that resides in every human being. It is a network of relationships focusing on balancing the production and consumption of art, and sharing this with the community with the intention to incubate a healthy and sustainable culture.

Burning Man, 2019

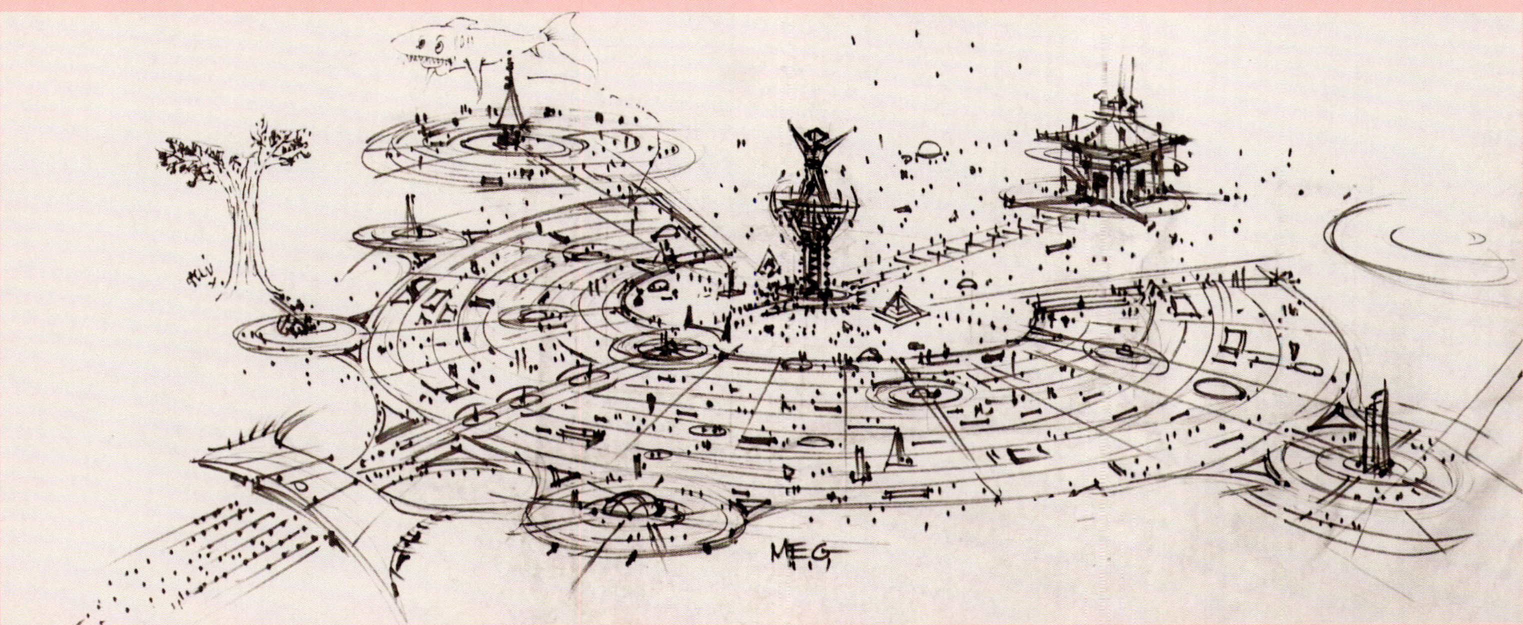

Burning Man original sketch, 2019

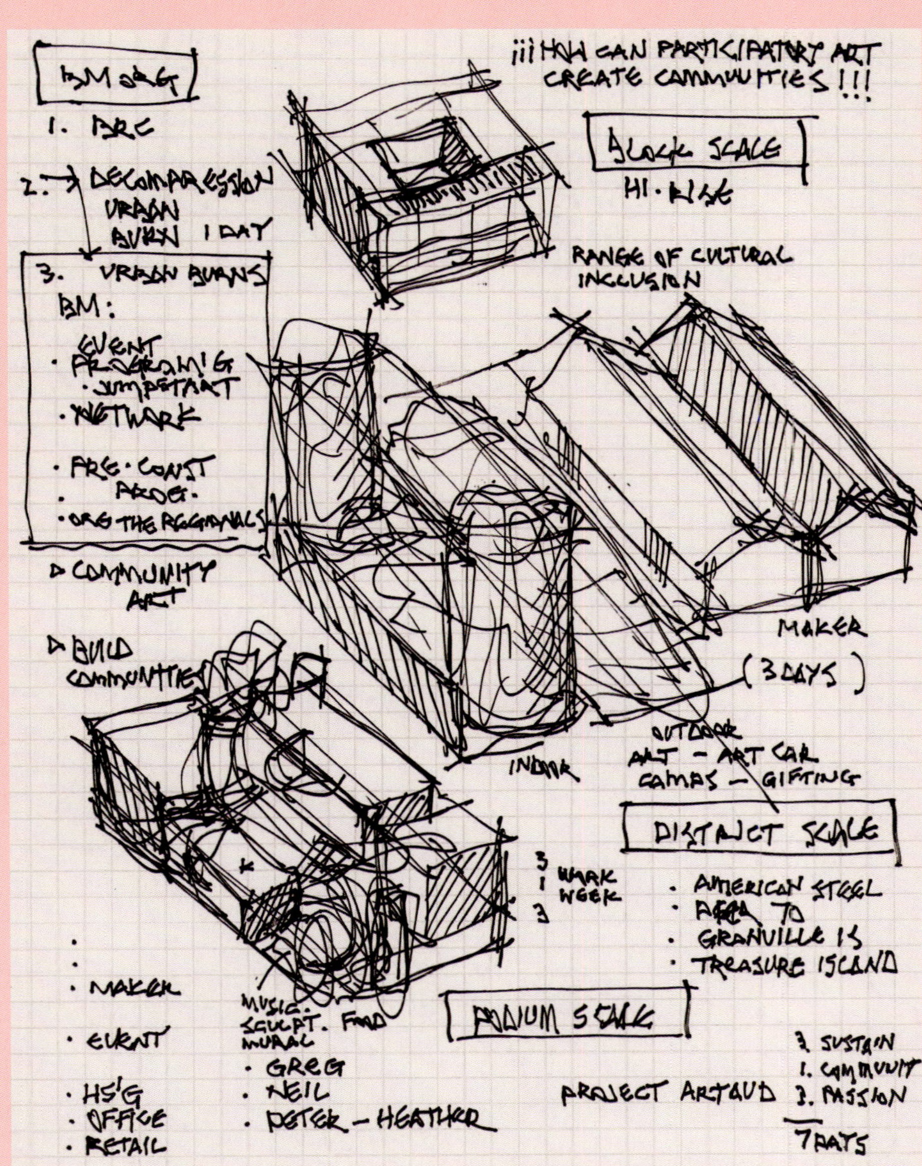

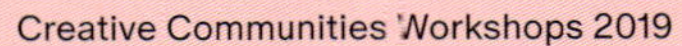
Creative Communities Workshops 2019

Burning Man Convening, Community Workshops at Esalen, CA, and Freiberg, Germany, 2019

6 Études

The poetry of dreams

"The essential point is that in the context of architecture the very act of free self-expression is inherently critical. And taking this idea further, because the vast majority of the drawings produced in architecture today are computer-made, to draw or paint by hand, as Marx himself does, is in itself a doubly critical act ... If buildings are to be capable of realizing these noble aspirations, then, as Marx's watercolours show us, drawing critically might be the means."

—Owen Hopkins, Senior Curator at Sir John Soane's Museum, London

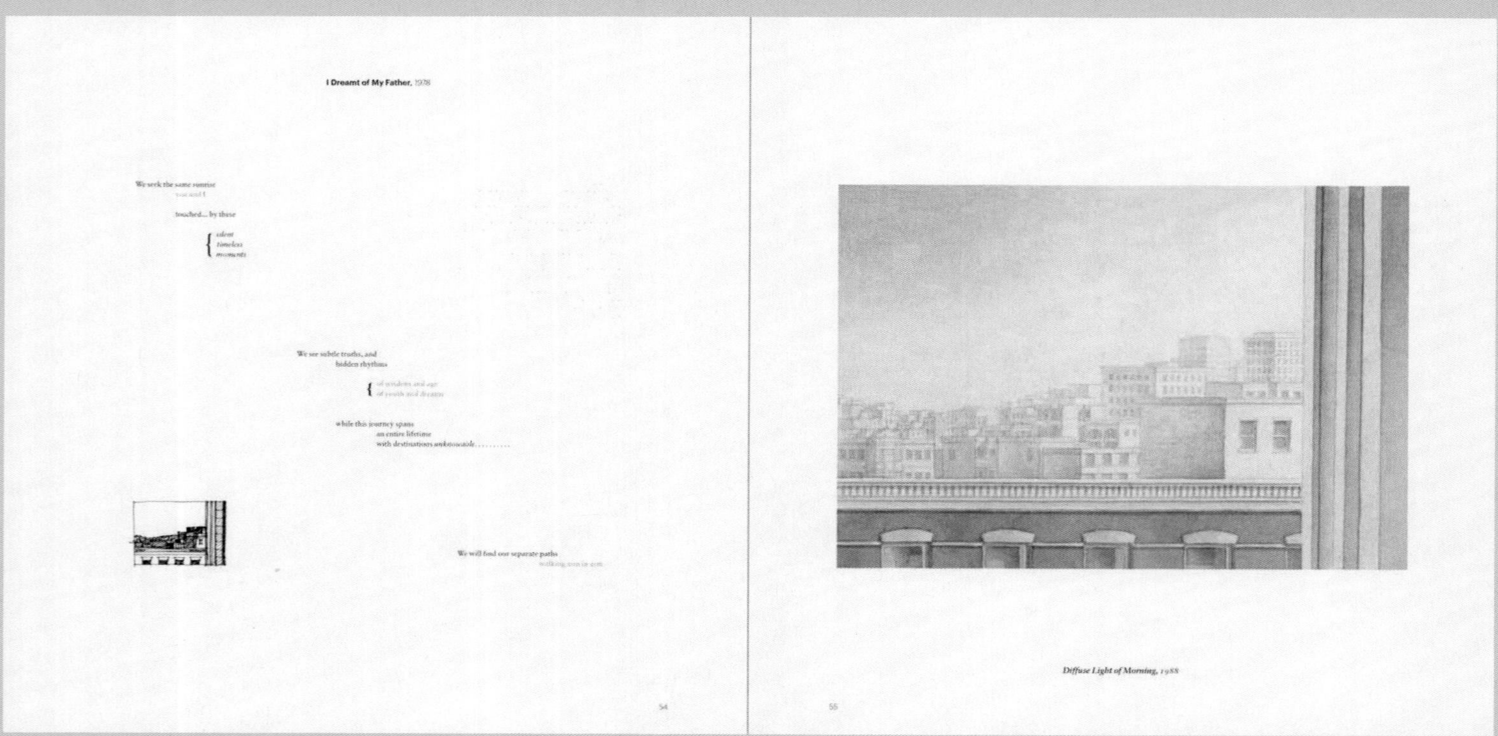

“There is a sense of condensed observation and acceptance of life, and humility in the face of beauty, in his poetry which accompanies John’s abstracted and refined watercolours—words flowing in space as thoughts journey across the pages ...”

—Ian Ritchie, CBE RA RIBA, Director of Ian Ritchie Architects Ltd

“John Marx is that comparative rarity: an architect whose working method is informed by his poetry. His paintings live somewhere in between poem and building —generated from ideas about space and time, enriched by colour, form, and the prospect of things to come.”

—Paul Finch, Editorial Director, *The Architectural Review*

The Museum of No Spectators at the 2023 Venice Biennale, Palazzo Mora

7 Architecture of Abundance

"Towards Abundance: The Delightful Paradoxes of Gender" advocates for designers and architects to reconsider a normative masculine tradition in how spaces are conceived and created, a tradition that may feel outdated yet is very much alive in contemporary practice. The monograph addresses the subject of gender and architectural design through multiple interpretations from a nonprescriptive, wholly inquisitive, and intellectually inclusive perspective.

Topics covered include: multicultural urbanism in the face of placeless and often characterless modernity; the introduction of a more sensual and sensitive placemaking that is welcoming to all; rethinking the singular maestro-led vision of how architecture is made; the paradox and evolution of vision and collaboration, especially in terms of gender norms; the types and qualities of gender categories; and male violence and normative design practice.

An overarching theme that resonates throughout the chapters is that of finding a better balance between the rational and the notional. The publication includes contributions by Adam Nathaniel Furman, Madelon Vriesendorp, Jessica Andrews, Pol Esteve Castelló, Dang Qun, Yael Reisner, Darran Anderson, Sumayya Vally, and many more.

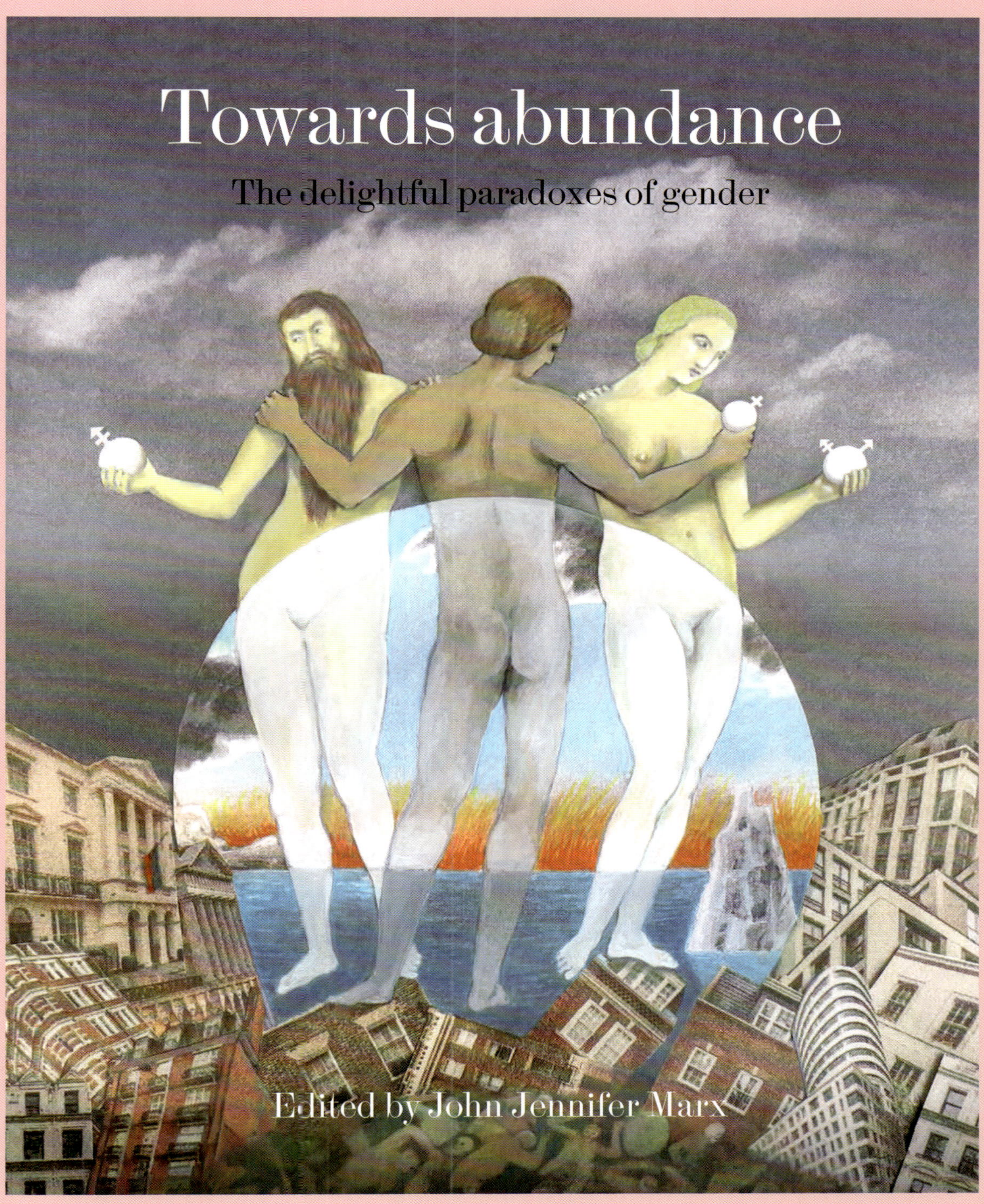

In Recognition for Advocacy and Architectural Poetics

American Prize for Architecture 2017

"These may well be the ultimate, true romantic architects."

“This ideal and its philosophy conveys a ‘vision of the future’ and all the artistic possibilities of imagination, emotional meaning, and lyrical expressionism for a consequential better and more enlightened world around us.”

“This year’s public accolade to this San Francisco office is significant in that it celebrates an architecture that inspires us, while celebrating the human condition and acknowledging the true sensitive requirements of a better designed and natural environment.”

“Form4 Architecture’s work pairs emotional and artistic substance to public and environmental placemaking and space-creating. Their practice focuses on the dynamics of form as the carrier of more lofty intent than just simply ‘building’.”

“Through an aggressive turning and twisting of organic architectural forms, the firm has passionately dedicated itself to the renewal of beauty in architecture and all its tangible and intangible forms. The firm rightly understands that Great Architecture must be as lyrical as it is functional.”

—Christian Narkiewicz-Laine

A single drop of water falls silently thru space thru the emptiness of existence thru the void in my dreams on its journey towards embracing the pristine a pool of water tranquil and pure Now...at impact becoming the pool rippling outwards its essence echoes from stone wall

to stone wall until its whisper is too faint for my ears This is the poetry of nothingness and everything you only need this one moment to understand the whole of the universe if you listen without intention the stillness will find...you

Author

John Jennifer Marx, AIA, is a cofounding principal and chief artistic officer of Form4 Architecture in San Francisco, California. He is responsible for developing Form4 Architecture's design vision and philosophical language. In order to return a sense of humanity back into architecture, he advocates for the inclusion of philosophy, art, and poetry in the thoughtful making of place by creating emotionally resonant architecture and urban spaces. He is a student of absurdity, paradox, kindness, and art.

John's design work and writing have been published in over 100 national and international publications. In 2018, the *Architectural Review* published his monograph "The Absurdity of Beauty: Rebalancing the Modernist Narrative." He has widely lectured on the topics of design, placemaking, emotional meaning and cultural vibrancy in Silicon Valley and places as diverse as South Korea, Italy, Austria, Australia, Canada, and Israel.

Form4 Architecture has received over 230 design awards and, in 2017, John became a Laureate of the American Prize for Architecture. Curated by The Chicago Athenaeum and The European Centre for Architecture, the award is recognized nationally and internationally as one of America's highest public tributes for architecture in the United States. The American Prize for Architecture is bestowed to an "outstanding practitioner in the United States that has emblazoned a new direction in the history of American Architecture with talent, vision, and commitment and has demonstrated consistent contributions to humanity through the built environment and through the art of architecture." The Chicago Athenaeum president cited Form4's "'vision of the future' and all the artistic possibilities of imagination, emotional meaning, and lyrical expressionism for a consequential better and more enlightened world around us."

He also won the 2017 Upstart Award, which honors the most innovative, disruptive, and creative business professionals throughout the San Francisco Bay Area.

John served on the board of the Magic Theatre in San Francisco from 2009 through 2020 and was its chair over five years. The Magic Theatre honored him with the Sam Shephard Legacy Award in 2018. John served on the board of the San Francisco Art Institute, one of the oldest and most prestigious art schools in the United States, from 2020 to 2023, with two years as co-chair.

The European Cultural Centre showed John Jennifer Marx's work at the Venice Architecture Biennale in Italy in 2016. In 2018, they exhibited his research "2nd Century Modernism: Reflections on Abundance," in both Venice and Moscow. In 2021, John exhibited his watercolors and poetry at Palazzo Mora during the Venice Biennale. In 2023, the Museum of No Spectators was the subject of an exhibition at the Palazzo Mora. The museum is currently located at Art City in Tucumcari, New Mexico.

In 2020, ORO Editions published an award-winning book entitled *Études: The Poetry of Dreams + Other Fragments*. This book focuses on 84 of John's watercolor paintings as well as 42 poems. In 2020, *Études* won an Indie Book Award for Illustration, and in 2021, John received the James Gates Percival International Prize for Literature. The Prize commemorates and pays tribute to the American Poet James Gates Percival (1795–1856) who is considered America's first poet shortly after the Revolutionary War.

In 2023, John Jennifer Marx edited an advocacy monograph with *The Architectural Review* on gender entitled "Towards Abundance: The Delightful Paradoxes of Gender," which debuted during the 2023 Venice Biennale. This publication seeks to deeply explore issues of gender in design, and how gender norms currently restrain the profession from fully embracing an inclusive world.

John has been going to Burning Man since 2015 and has also written about the importance of its participatory culture with regard to the design process and as a catalyst for social change. He has participated as a poet in poetry readings, as an artist—creating wearable art collages—and was the architect and co-lead artist on two art projects.

Originally from the Midwest, John has lived in San Francisco since 1981, with his wife Nikki Beach who is an internationally sought-after maker of architectural model trees. They share a home designed by John and inspired by the painter Piet Mondrian.

About Form4

Form4 is a unique firm in our commitment to the balance of three things: extending the range of cultural inclusion, advocating for humanism and emotional meaning, and artistically exploring lyrical expressionism. It is our ambition to respond to the spirit of our times relative to the notion that **architecture has disengaged with society** and is losing its cultural relevance.

We are embracing a fundamental change in the way architects design, with the intention of rebalancing modernism toward an architecture of emotional abundance, adding to its current focus on an architecture of abstraction and ideas. This involves rebalancing the role of emotional meaning in design intent, as well as evaluating the impact of what we create on the public at large.

Form4 is a **Second Century Modernist** firm where we measure success by our contributions to society as we balance expressive design, rigor, empathy, and sustainability to create captivating buildings and spaces that resonate with people and enhance their lives. In our exploration of emotional meaning, we find that **the most sustainable things in life are those things you won't throw away because you love them too much**. In a sense, you will fight for and preserve the things you love.

Our advocacy has taken 10 paths:

1 Emotional Meaning—Visual Poems
The Architect's Newspaper 2015
Venice Biennale 2016

2 "The Absurdity of Beauty: Rebalancing the Modernist Narrative," *The Architectural Review* 2018

3 Second Century Modernism
Venice Biennale 2018
Moscow 2019

4 Cultural Vibrancy
Burning Man 2015–Present

5 Creative Community Workshops
Esalen 2019
Freiburg 2019
Italian Pavilion, Venice Biennale 2021

6 Art is an Essential Service (Covid)
Études: The Poetry of Dreams, ORO Editions 2020
Venice Biennale 2021

7 Gender in Design
"Towards Abundance: The Delightful Paradoxes of Gender," *The Architectural Review* 2023
Abitare 2023
Pecha Kucha, Design Museum 2024

8 Embracing Paradox
Common Edge
WAF 2024

9 AI/Metaverse
10 articles for *ArchDaily*

10 Memoir + Monograph
Machine Books
ORO Editions

"In order to return a sense of humanity to design, we advocate for a rebalancing of modernism with emotional meaning and poetic design."

Project credits

LYRICAL EXPRESSIONISM

Intertwined Eternities
Location: Aptos, California, United States
Year: Designed 2021
Client: Episcopal Church of St. John the Baptist
Design team:
Form4 Architecture
John Marx, AIA, Project Designer and Chief Artistic Officer
Paul Ferro, Principal in Charge and CEO
Cullen Taub, Project Architect
Saba Raji, Designer

Falling Lotus Blossoms
Location: Pune, India
Year: 2015
Client: Panchshil Realty
Design team:
Form4 Architecture,
John Marx, AIA, Project Designer, Principal in Charge, and Chief Artistic Officer
NPAPL Architects, Executive Architect

Portal of the Winds
Location: Jeju, South Korea
Year: Designed 2003
Client: Jung-il Architects
Design team:
Form4 Architecture
John Marx, AIA, Project Designer, Principal in Charge, and Chief Artistic Officer

Crashing Waves
Location: Tongyeong, South Korea
Year: Designed 2009
Client: Donghee Oh, Gansam Architects and Partners
Design team:
John Marx, AIA, Project Designer, Principal in Charge, and Chief Artistic Officer
John Fisher, AIA, John Sergio Fisher & Associates Inc., Theatre Architect/Theatre Consultant and Planner

Lyrical Seashore
Location: True Love River Harbor, Kaohsiung Harbor, Taiwan
Year: 2010
Client: Barry Cheng Architect @ Kaohsiung
Design team:
Form4 Architecture
John Marx, AIA, Project Designer, Principal in Charge, and Chief Artistic Officer

Sanguine Lily
Location: Dublin, Ireland
Year: Designed 2013
Client: RIAI Awards and Competition
Design team:
Form4 Architecture
John Marx, AIA, Project Designer, Principal in Charge, and Chief Artistic Officer

Glass Butterfly
Location: Holbaek, Denmark
Year: Designed 2013
Client: Innosite
Design team:
Form4 Architecture
John Marx, AIA, Project Designer, Principal in Charge, and Chief Artistic Officer

Poet's Journey
Location: Galena, Illinois, United States
Year: Designed 2019
Client: The Chicago Athenaeum: Museum of Architecture and Design and The European Centre for Architecture Art Design and Urban Studies
Design team:
Form4 Architecture
John Marx, AIA, Project Designer, Principal in Charge, and Chief Artistic Officer

House of Borrowed Light
Location: San Francisco, CA United States
Year: 2005
Client: Brandon Wang
Design team:
Form4 Architecture
John Marx, AIA, Project Designer, Principal in Charge, and Chief Artistic Officer

Sea Song
Location: Big Sur, California, United States
Year: Designed 2014–2018
Client: Confidential
Design team:
Form4 Architecture John Marx, AIA, Project Designer, Principal in Charge, and Chief Artistic Officer

Luminous Moon Gate
Location: Taichung Gateway Park, Park Avenue 2, Taichung, Taiwan
Year: 2013
Developer/Client: Barry Cheng @Taichung City
Design team:
Form4 Architecture
John Marx, AIA, Project Designer, Principal in Charge, and Chief Artistic Officer
Pierluigi Serraino, AIA (Team)
Felix Lin (Team)

Cloudscape
Location: San Francisco, California, United States
Year: Designed 2019
Client: Trammell Crow Company, Peter Brandon
Design team:
Form4 Architecture
John Marx, AIA, Project Designer, Principal in Charge, and Chief Artistic Officer

Innovation Curve
Location: Palo Alto, California, United States
Year: 2020
Client: Sand Hill Property Company
Design team:
Form4 Architecture
John Marx, AIA, Project Designer and Chief Artistic Officer
Robert Giannini, Principal in Charge
James Tefend, Principal/Project Manager
Consultants:
Studio Five Design (Landscape Architect)
Luminae Souter (Lighting Designer)
DCI, Inc. (Structural Engineer)
M-E Engineers (MEP Engineer)
BKF (Civil Engineers)

WARM MODERNISM

Where The Birds Sing
Location: Palo Alto, California, United States
Year: 2017
Client: VMware
Design team:
Form4 Architecture
John Marx, AIA, Project Designer and Chief Artistic Officer
Robert Giannini, Partner in Charge
Paul Ferro, Project Manager, Renovation Projects
James Tefend, Project Manager, New Projects
Interior Architect: Form4 Architecture
Consultants:
PWP Landscape Architecture (Landscape Architects (Phase 2))
Studio Five Design (Landscape Architects (Phase 3))
Swinerton Builders (General Contractor)
Adapture Structural Engineering (Structural Engineer)
Louie International (Structural Engineer)
BKF (Civil Engineer)
M-E Engineers (Mechanical/Electrical Engineer)

Layered Grace
Location: Los Gatos, California, United States
Year: 2015
Client: Sand Hill Property Company
Design team:
Form4 Architecture
John Marx, AIA, Project Designer and Chief Artistic Officer
Robert Giannini, Principal in Charge
James Tefend, Principal/Project Manager
Consultants:
Studio Five Design (Landscape Architect)
Arup, Inc. (Lighting Designer, Theater Design)
DCI, Inc. (Structural Engineer)
M-E Engineers (MEP Engineer)
Shen Milson Wilke (Acoustical Consultant)

Overlaid Harmonies
Location: Redwood City, California, United States
Year: 2018
Client: Premia Capital
Design team:
Form4 Architecture
John Marx, AIA, Project Designer and Chief Artistic Officer
Robert Giannini, Principal in Charge
James Tefend, Principal/Project Manager
Consultants:
The Guzzardo Partnership (Landscape Architect)
Ecological Building Strategies (Sustainability)
South Bay Construction (General Contractor)
BKF Engineers (Civil Engineer)
Holmes Cully (Structural Engineer)
Energy Soft (Energy Model)
Simpson Gumpertz & Heger (Waterproofing)
Luminae (Lighting Design)

Mondrian's Window
Location: San Francisco, California, United States
Year: 2014
Client: John Marx and Nikki Beach
Design team:
Form4 Architecture
John Marx, AIA, Project Designer, Principal in Charge, and Chief Artistic Officer
Ho Man Wong, Project Architect
Nathan Reasons, Job Captain

Urban Frames
Location: Palo Alto, California, United States
Year: Designed 2015
Client: CM Capital
Design team:
Form4 Architecture
John Marx, AIA, Project Designer and Chief Artistic Officer
Robert Giannini, Principal in Charge

DYNAMIC BALANCE

Folded Wings
Location: Palo Alto, California, United States
Year: 2020
Client: Sand Hill Property Company
Design team:
Form4 Architecture
John Marx, AIA, Project Designer and Chief Artistic Officer
Robert Giannini, Principal in Charge
James Tefend, Principal/Project Manager
Jongho Park, Designer
Consultants:
Studio Five Design (Landscape Architect)
BKF (Civil Engineers)
M-E Engineers (MEP Engineer)
DCI, Inc. (Structural Engineer)
Truebeck Construction (General Construction)
Sage Green (LEED Consulting)

Sub-urban Canyon
Location: Santa Clara, California, United States
Year: 2008
Client: The Sobrato Organization
Design team:
Form4 Architecture
John Marx, AIA, Project Designer and Chief Artistic Officer
Robert Giannini, Principal in Charge

Oasis
Location: Santa Clara, California, United States
Year: Designed 2011
Client: The Sobrato Organization
Design team:
Form4 Architecture
John Marx, AIA, Project Designer and Chief Artistic Officer
Robert Giannini, Principal in Charge

Resonance
Location: Silicon Valley, California, United States
Year: Designed 2017
Client: Trammell Crow Company, Peter Brandon

Design team:
Form4 Architecture
John Marx, AIA, Project Designer, Principal in Charge and Chief Artistic Officer

Campus X
Location: Santa Clara, California, United States
Year: 2016
Client: Trammell Crow Company, Peter Brandon
Design team:
Form4 Architecture
John Marx, AIA, Project Designer, Principal in Charge, and Chief Artistic Officer

Binary Harmonics
Location: Oakland, California, United States
Year: Designed 2018
Client: Trammell Crow Company, Peter Brandon
Design team:
Form4 Architecture
John Marx, AIA, Project Designer, Principal in Charge, and Chief Artistic Officer

Corten Ribbon
Location: Walnut Creek, California, United States
Year: 2020
Client: Hines
Design team:
Form4 Architecture
John Marx, AIA, Project Designer and Chief Artistic Officer
Paul Ferro, Principal in Charge and CEO
Pauline Malaquin, Designer
Jericho Edwards, Designer
Consultants:
Form4 Architecture (Interior Designer)
Environmental Foresight, Inc. (Landscape Architect)
KPFF Consulting Engineers (Structural Engineer)
Kier + Wright (Civil Engineer)
Salter (Acoustical Designer)
NOVO Construction (General Contractor)

Verdant Sanctuary
Location: Palo Alto, California, United States
Year: Designed 2022
Client: Sand Hill Property Company
Design team:
Form4 Architecture
John Marx, Project Designer and Chief Artistic Officer
James Tefend, Principal in Charge
Jongho Park, Designer
Consultants:
Guzzardo Partnership (Landscape Architect)
Luminae Souter (Lighting Designer)
DCI, Inc. (Structural Engineer)
M-E Engineers (MEP Engineer)
BKF (Civil Engineers)

ADVOCACY

Andromeda Reimagined
Location: Black Rock City, Nevada, United States
Year: Designed 2019
Client: Self-Initiated
Design Team:
John Marx, Architect/Lead Artist, Form4 Architecture, Project Designer
Brian Poindexter, Producer/Visionary (Team)
Consultants:
Derrick Roorda, Buro Happold (Structural Engineer)
Mary Graham, paintings (Artist)
Mischell Riley, “Freedom and Awaken” (Artist)
John Marx (Poetry)

Museum of No Spectators
Location: Black Rock City, Nevada, United States
Year: 2022
Client: Self-Initiated
Design team:
Form4 Architecture
John Marx, AIA, Design Architect and Co-Lead Artist, Principal in Charge, and Chief Artistic Officer
Natalia Cervantes, Designer
Collaborators:
Absinthia Vermut (Co-Lead Artist)
Lonnie Graham (Head Curator/Director of Cultural Inclusion)
Wes Skinner (Lead Builder/Welder)
James Monday (Project Manager)
Paul Delathauwer (Gifting Shop Director)
Derrick Roorda, Buro Happold (Structural Engineer)
YZZO Studios (Steel Fabrication)

Golden Cage
Location: Black Rock City, Nevada, United States
Year: Designed 2019
Client: Burning Man Project
Design Team:
Form4 Architecture
John Marx, Project Designer, Principal in Charge, and Chief Artistic Officer

Human Convergence
Location: San Jose, California, United States
Year: Designed 2020
Client: Urban Confluence Silicon Valley
Design team:
Form4 Architecture
John Marx, AIA, Project Designer, Principal in Charge, and Chief Artistic Officer

The Portal
Location: Reno, Nevada, United States
Year: Designed 2024
Client: REGENESIS Reno
Design team:
Form4 Architecture
John Marx, AIA, Project Designer, Principal in Charge, and Chief Artistic Officer
Jongho Park, Designer

Image credits

LYRICAL EXPRESSIONISM

Intertwined Eternities
Renderings by Form4 Architecture / Downtown

Falling Lotus Blossoms
Photos by Craig Auckland FOTOHAUS / Pixeldo Media / Navdeep Soni / TerraServer

Portal of the Winds
Renderings by Form4 Architecture / Downtown

Crashing Waves
Renderings by Form4 Architecture / Downtown

Lyrical Seashore
Renderings by Form4 Architecture / Downtown

Sanguine Lily
Renderings by Form4 Architecture / Downtown

Glass Butterfly
Renderings by Form4 Architecture / Downtown

A Poet's Journey
Renderings by Form4 Architecture / Teapot Collective

House of Borrowed Light
Photos by JD Peterson

Sea Song
Renderings by Form4 Architecture / Downtown

Luminous Moon Gate
Renderings by Form4 Architecture / Downtown

Cloudscape
Renderings by Form4 Architecture / Downtown

Innovation Curve
Photos by Richard Barnes / John Sutton Photography

WARM MODERNISM

Where the Birds Sing
Photos by John Sutton Photography

Layered Grace
Photos by Frank Paul Perez Architectural & Commercial Photographer

Overlaid Harmonies
Photos by John Sutton Photography

Mondrian's Window
Photos by Bruce Damonte Photography, Inc. / John Jennifer Marx

Urban Frames
Renderings by Form4 Architecture / Downtown

DYNAMIC BALANCE

Folded Wings
Photos by John Sutton Photography

Sub-Urban Canyon
Renderings by Form4 Architecture / Downtown

Oasis
Renderings by Form4 Architecture / Downtown

Resonance
Renderings by Form4 Architecture / Downtown

Campus X
Renderings by Form4 Architecture / Downtown

Binary Harmonics
Renderings by Form4 Architecture / Teapot Collective

Corten Ribbon
Photos by John Sutton Photography

Verdant Sanctuary
Renderings by Form4 Architecture / Teapot Collective

ADVOCACY

Andromeda Reimagined
Photos by Hannu Rytky / John Jennifer Marx

Museum of No Spectators
Photos by Lonnie Graham / John Jennifer Marx / Hannu Rytky / Absinthia Vermut

Golden Cage
Renderings by John Jennifer Marx and Downtown

Human Convergence
Renderings by Form4 Architecture / Downtown

The Portal
Renderings by Form4 Architecture / Downtown / Teapot Collective

4	Rendering by Form4 Architecture/Downtown
7	Lucia Moholy, Bauhaus-Gebäude Dessau, 1925–1926, Blick auf das Werkstattgebäude von Nordwesten, 1926, Bauhaus-Archiv Berlin / © VG Bild-Kunst, Bonn
9	Rendering by Form4 Architecture/Downtown
10	Top: Eugène Viollet-le-Duc, Paris Opera House, 1861, public domain Bottom: Ludwig Hilberseimer, Highrise City (Hochhausstadt): Perspective View: North-South Street, 1924
14	John Jennifer Marx with Jeremy Mende
20	John Jennifer Marx with Jeremy Mende
21	Ludwig Hilberseimer, Highrise City (Hochhausstadt): Perspective View: North-South Street, 1924
23	Mark Luthringer
25	Carol M. Highsmith/Library of Congress
32	Mark Luthringer
36–37	John Jennifer Marx with Jeremy Mende
41	Pierluigi Serraino
44	Rendering by Form4 Architecture/Downtown
45-46	John Jennifer Marx with Jeremy Mende
48–50	John Jennifer Marx with Jeremy Mende
51	Bottom: Photo by Crimson Rose
52	John Jennifer Marx with Jeremy Mende
53	Gabor Gallov
241	John Jennifer Marx with Jeremy Mende
242	European Cultural Center
243	*The Architectural Review*
246	Will Rogers
249	Top: John Sutton Bottom: European Cultural Center
251	Madelon Vriesendorp and *The Architectural Review*
252	*The Architectural Review*

Colophon

ORO Editions
Publishers of Architecture, Art, and Design
Gordon Goff: Publisher

www.oroeditions.com
info@oroeditions.com

Published by ORO Editions

Author: John Jennifer Marx
Editor: Original Copy
Book Design: StudioSpass
Project Manager: Jake Anderson

10 9 8 7 6 5 4 3 2 1 First Edition

ISBN: 978-1-957183-34-3

Prepress and Print work by ORO Editions Inc.
Printed in China

ORO Editions makes a continuous effort to minimize the overall carbon footprint of its publications. As part of this goal, ORO, in association with Global ReLeaf, arranges to plant trees to replace those used in the manufacturing of the paper produced for its books. Global ReLeaf is an international campaign run by American Forests, one of the world's oldest nonprofit conservation organizations. Global ReLeaf is American Forests' education and action program that helps individuals, organizations, agencies, and corporations improve the local and global environment by planting and caring for trees.

Acknowledgments

The Living:

The most important women in my life:
Nikki, Andrea, and Sarah

The Poets:
Ian Ritchie
Richard England
Christian + Kieran + Ioannis

The Architectural Review group:
Manon Mollard
Max Zarzycki
Jeremy Melvin
Paul Finch
Adam Nathanial Furman
Madelon Vriesendorp

The people who enable, support, and encourage this insanity:
Julie Taylor
Laura Iloniemi
Wendy Goodman

The deep artistic and intellectual collaborators:
Pierluigi Serraino
Jeremy Mende

The Playa Daughters and Venetian Muses:
Lucia, Elena, Sarah, Rachele ... and Valeria

My friends, artists, and fellow Students of Absurdity:
Kevin Klinger
Lonnie Graham
Matty Mo
James Monday
Francis Stefani
Colin Speer

My Form4 partners:
Bob Giannini
Paul Ferro
James Tefend

The Builders:
Wes Skinner
Poindexter
Michael Austin

The Technologists:
Yehuda Kalay
Chris Yessios

The exceptional clients:
Peter Brandon
Brandon Wang
Peter Pau + Allison Koo
John Shenk
The John Sobratos
Kevin Kim

The Creative Community:
Maya + Debi
Gordon Gossage
Ulrich Gehmann

The Futurists:
Peter Hirshberg
Barry Threw
Michael Maggio
Kent Larson

My design collaborators:
Jongho Park
Saba Raji
Pauline Malaquin
Arianna Deane

The Digital Artists and Poets:
Tomek Miksa
Joao David

The person who made this book possible: Gordon Goff

The Comfort Disruption and Creative Sweetness Team:
Jaron Korvinus + Daan Mens

The person who breathed life into this book project and stayed with it through Covid:
Julia van den Hout

The dead:

Architects who have deeply influenced my career and development as an artist and a human:
Bing Coney
Julie Maser
Warren Callister
Herb McLaughlin
Will Alsop